# What is Classicism?

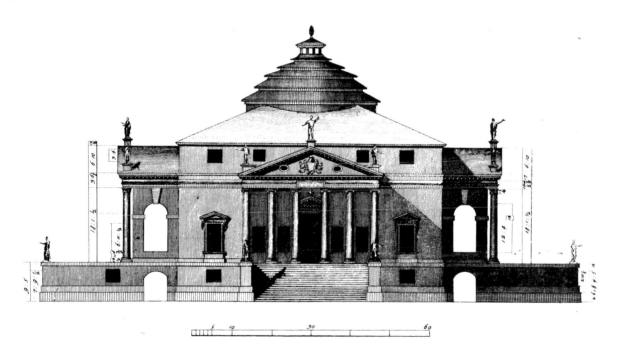

ANDREA PALLADIO, VILLA ROTUNDA, VICENZA, 1550s, DRAWING BY B SCAMOZZI, 1778

T HANSEN, ACADEMY IN ATHENS, DETAIL, 1859-87

MICHAEL GREENHALGH

# What is Classicism?

ACADEMY EDITIONS · LONDON/ST. MARTIN'S PRESS · NEW YORK

# Acknowledgements

We would like to thank the many architects who have given permission for reproduction of their works, and the following who have lent us their photographs: Demetri Porphyrios, pp6, 7, 64 and Back Cover; Liam O'Connor, p2; Michael Greenhalgh, pp12, 14, 15, 17, 41; Jean-Claude Gerlier, p32; Charles Jencks, pp18, 57; Allan Greenberg, p60; Witney Cox, p62. Works reproduced are from the following collections: Dulwich Picture Gallery, p21; Musée des Augustins, Toulouse, p26; Metropolitan Museum of Art, p27; The John Soane Museum (from *John Soane*, Academy), p33; Venturi, Scott Brown and Associates, p54; The Doria Gallery, Rome, p66; Helen Rosenau, *Boulée and Visionary Architecture* (Academy); p30; Gerard Legrand, *Giorgio de Chirico* (Academy), p37. All other material from Academy archives.

*FRONT COVER*: STIRLING WILFORD & ASSOCIATES, NEUE STAATSGALERIE, STUTTGART, 1984
*BACK COVER* : PROPYLAIA, ATHENS, 437-32BC

Published in Great Britain in 1990 by
ACADEMY EDITIONS
an imprint of the Academy Group Ltd, 7 Holland Street, London W8 4NA

Copyright © 1990 Academy Editions, London
*All rights reserved*
No part of this publication may be
reproduced in any manner whatsoever without
permission in writing from Academy Editions

ISBN 0-85670-970-0

Published in the United States of America by
ST. MARTIN'S PRESS,
175 Fifth Avenue, New York, NY 10010

ISBN 0-312-04925-0

Printed and bound in Singapore

# Contents

Introduction 7

Classicism: A Broad Definition 9

The Classical Tradition: Origins and Importance 12

Classicism: The Middle Ages and the Renaissance 13

Classicism in Medieval and Renaissance Architecture 16

The 17th Century 20

The 18th Century: History and Neo-Classicism 21

Classicism in Painting and Sculpture: 18th and 19th Centuries 24

Academies and Change 28

Neo-Classicism in 19th-Century Architecture 31

Classicism and the Battle of the Styles 34

Classicism in 20th-Century Painting and Sculpture 36

Modern Architecture and Classicism 38

Planning the Modern City 40

Modernism and Post-Modernism in Architecture 41

Post-Modernism and Historicism 50

Conclusion: Classicism, Post-Modernism and the Future 58

Epilogue 63

Notes 66

T HANSEN, ACADEMY IN ATHENS, FRONT PORTICO, 1859

# What is Classicism?

PARTHENON, ATHENS, 447-438 BC

**Introduction**

Why another book on Classicism? There are four main reasons. The first is concerned with the very heritage of European civilisation: the classical approach has played a considerable part in the complexion of the arts and of intellectual life in Europe for well over 2000 years, so that to understand the art entails understanding the ideals, applications and varieties of Classicism. The second is a broader argument: the structure of Classicism – namely a canon of qualities and ideals used again and again in a series of deliberate revivals – exists not just in Europe[1] and Europeanised parts of the world, or indeed in areas known to the Greeks and Romans as 'barbaric',[2] but in the East as well.[3] In other words, some of the concepts the term embodies may well be very widespread, if not universal. In China, for example, as in Imperial Rome, Powers believes that 'the authority for the "ideal" that became classical was derived from a past that was known chiefly through literary sources and works of art', and classicising art was used as a tool to 'prove' superiority over the previous dynasty:

the architecture and ceremonies of the previous dynasty were described as 'extravagant', 'tortuous', or 'confusing', whereas those of Emperor Ming were characterised as 'symmetrical', 'ordered', 'solemn', 'majestic', 'dignified', 'frugal', 'stately', 'restrained' and 'simple'; and he concludes:

If the term 'Classicism' is applied in this way to early China, then its essence must be found in a secular, historical thrust, in subject matter based on the classics, in association with moral ideals beneficial to the empire, and in the introduction of a new aesthetic based on an ideal of refined plainness.[4]

All these concepts are directly transferable into a European context, and are fruitful for our subsequent discussion – complication to simplicity, extravagance to order, and so on – together with their political dimension. The 'historical thrust' of which Powers writes is certainly a main feature of Classicism, as is an emphasis on morality, on Empire (in the widest sense – Papal and Imperial), on textual tradition and on a new aesthetic. It is certainly true that Classicism itself is an authoritarian tradition, peculiarly fitted to the expression of political and dynastic superiority. And indeed, it may be that an interest in certain sets of perceived qualities in the arts of the past, and the uses made of such interest in later centuries, is a valuable part of artistic evolution in those many cultures where tradition itself is valued and where, in consequence, it is the values of the past which form the basis for the re-interpreted values of the present – I use the word *values*, and not simply styles or motifs, advisedly. As George Hersey observes[5] of Graeco-Roman Classicism, it 'was not only the architecture of the Greeks and Romans and of their empires, it was also the architecture, *mutatis mutandis*, of Romanesque Europe and of Byzantium, of the Renaissance and the Baroque, Beaux-Arts, and fascism; it is even, in a peculiar but strong way, a contributor to Post-Modernism' – which leaves little outside the classicising equation except for Barbarism, Gothic and Romanticism. Much the same applies in painting and sculpture. By studying the development of Classicism, then, we can learn more not only about the very nature of the art and architecture of the past (and hence the present), but also about our forbears' attitudes and ideas.

The third reason brings the first one up-to-date, so to speak: with the current debates on Post-Modernism, principally but not exclusively in architecture, Classicism is again perceived by many to be an interesting issue which has once more brought questions of architecture before the public eye, so that any treatment of it (especially by a contemporary architect) is likely to be not simply descriptive and historical, but prescriptive as well. Thirty years ago one might have believed that Classicism was dead, destroyed with the ashes of those National Socialist and Fascist monuments in Germany and Italy which apparently provided such an embarrassing demonstration of how Classicism could be used to political and propagandistic ends. Today, as we shall see below, Classicism is promoted by some as a vital aid in setting the arts back on The Right Path – rather than, as used to be the case, as an outmoded and near-dead survival redolent of the quirks of the academies, and not at all 'modern'. Such a volte-face in the space of a generation should teach us how fickle are artistic fashions – especially when seen against the perennial vigour of Classicism.

The fourth reason is that, since the Second World War, study of the classical heritage and knowledge of the subject continues to broaden our horizons, as art-historians realise that artists and architects in previous centuries had good access to a range of antique artefacts much richer and broader than was once realised; and that, consequently, we have to look much further afield than simply Italy or indeed Western Europe in order to ascertain what was notionally available.[6] Taking the longer and broader view, this is precisely what Classicism is always about – namely the revival and re-working of past ideas and styles, and their fitting to modern

circumstances. Ideas are important – much more important than mere motifs, which cannot receive the oxygen of acceptance without the understanding of successive generations of what motifs actually meant – or, at least, what new meanings they can bear. As Leon Krier defines the term for architecture, classical work is 'based on the fundamental principles of *venustas, firmitas, utilitas*; translated into modern language as harmony-beauty, stability-permanence, utility-comfort'.[7] And Beauty, as Saint Augustine reminds us, is the splendour of Truth.

In other words, forms are the carriers of meanings, and often powerful meanings at that. Frequently, the meanings cannot be precisely stated in words, for it is after all part of the mission of art and architecture to express meanings other than by words. This book will demonstrate that only rarely has the ideal of Classicism been applied without some attendant ideology; hence that Classicism is not merely a range of styles, but rather a way of perceiving the world and using the arts to persuade others to see it in a similar fashion.

In order to elucidate these points, this book will examine in brief outline the history of the classical tradition, as a way of explaining its tenacity and longevity. Because it is a robust tradition (and not just an ephemeral movement), and because it is far from monolithic, Classicism must be studied in the context of its changing meaning, and this demands an historical approach. Particular attention will be given to 19th and 20th century developments. With the public debate provoked by post-modernist architecture (a development of the last 20 years), the whole matter of Classicism and its relevance is once more before the public eye – gainsaying those who believed it to be a dead issue.

The tradition of Classicism will be presented not as a conglomeration of styles, but rather as a set of agreed values which were integral to European society from late Antiquity through to the early 19th century, and which are still of use. The approach I follow is both thematic and chronological, although it cannot of course be exhaustive. Beginning with a definition of the terminology and with a very brief survey of the reasons for the longevity of the classical tradition and its prestige in earlier centuries, the book then deals with how that ideal affects productions in painting, sculpture and architecture from Antiquity to the 18th century, the period which is chosen and explained as initiating a watershed between Renaissance and modern traditions. Further to underline the changing nature of the topic, and following a prospectus on Classicism in modern times, the book concludes with an updated definition of the term which fits the changed circumstances of our century.

A book as short as this cannot aim to be comprehensive either in scope or in detail; however, it attempts to include much of the important recent literature of the subject. For a classified bibliography of over 1,000 items on the subject from late Antiquity to Ingres, see my 'The Classical Tradition' in *Art*, London 1978. Naturally, because of the breadth of the subject, no bibliography of Classicism or its tradition can hope to be comprehensive; the consolation is that the leads provided in the notes should allow you to double or triple your reading should you so wish. This book differs from *The Classical Tradition* not only in length, but also in that it continues the story beyond Ingres, giving almost half the text to the various forms of Classicism from the later 19th century up to the present day, and emphasising architecture much more than painting and sculpture.

## Classicism: A Broad Definition

The first task in discussing definitions is to emphasise that the very terms *Classicism* and *classical tradition* are not precise ones. There is no general agreement on one suitable definition, because the words themselves are capable of several interpretations depending on the context. Indeed, they were constantly redefined by devotees throughout the centuries, so that the meaning changed – and this, the very desire to redefine terms of continuing importance for contemporary life, so as to view them from new perspectives, is one of the reasons for the longevity of the ideas they encapsulate. The changing meaning of Classicism for Goethe and Schiller (tinged as it is with romanticism) is a case in point.[8]

One meaning of *classical* is as a kind of shorthand reference to the work of a certain period of acknowledged excellence within Antiquity, conventionally from the Persian Invasion of 490BC to Philip of Macedon in 338BC.[9] But this is indeed shorthand, for here a pseudo-stylistic label is being given to a period which is defined by external events. Of course there are family resemblances among the arts of this period, but the differences are also great. The term is preserved because it is convenient, not because it is a historically or stylistically accurate formulation to explain the complexity of what actually happened.

This use of the term to characterise one period has also been almost endlessly enlarged, first to denote revivals of that Classicism, such as in the Rome of Augustus, but then to encompass the whole of Graeco-Roman Antiquity, so that the expression *classical antiquity* would not raise an eyebrow; and when *classics* are studied as a subject, the usual understanding is also of the period from the rise of Greece to the fall of Rome. Nowadays, however, *Classicism* can also be used to designate *modern* periods, especially that of the late 18th and early 19th centuries, sometimes called Neo-Classicism.[10]

To add to the confusion, *classical* is also used even more generally, as a shorthand way of referring to work of the highest quality, and not to style. Indeed, this usage either ignores style, or cheerfully incorporates works which are by no stretch of the imagination classical. So the novels of Jane Austen or the works of Mozart might be called *classics,* but here the term is used to indicate only that they are of recognised excellence – as with Western classical music, Indian classical music, classical African sculpture, or classical Arab Islam. Although some authors will find a 'classical equilibrium' in all such productions,[11] it is but rarely that they bear any relation either to Antiquity or to classical values in the broader sense. Hence a 'classic' need not be in any sense *classical*. Which underlines a previous point: although the discussion of Classicism will, in this book, be restricted to Western Europe, characteristics associated with the classical tradition (including, sometimes, style) are discernible further East, as we have already seen.

But is all antique art and architecture *classical* by virtue of the period in which it was made? Is work produced in Italy during the High Renaissance classical by virtue of its one style (rather than its quality)? Surely not, because of the complexity of both (and indeed all other) ages. Periodisation gives us rough and ready convenience: it is accurate neither as an intellectual nor as a stylistic label. The problems do not stop here, for if we put together the notions of 'recognised excellence' and 'tradition' it is clear that there are productions in all the arts which are classical in this broad sense, but not in the narrower one – that is, which have no connection either with the art of ancient Greece or Rome, or with the strong traditions deriving from it. The plays of Shakespeare would be one example, Gothic architecture another – although it can be argued that the latter is but a brief interval in the subtle reign of Classicism. Perspectives change according to place and time; and it will be as well to bear in mind that different countries have different traditions and, indeed, different 'flavours' or interpretations of the classical. The east facade of the Louvre would have looked just as strange to Bramante as the Pantheon to Ictinus, so we might say that all works tend to be classical only within restricted areas – which is surely less biased than the usual device of taking the yardstick of – say – the Italian Renaissance by which to measure the productions of other countries.

So should we take a strict or a latitudinarian view of what is classical? A very narrow definition would quickly turn into an exercise of separating the sheep from the goats: is all Raphael's work classical, for example? And none of Caravaggio's?[12] What about Bernini, and the Baroque in general? Or about terms such as *romantic Classicism*? For were not some Romantics classical? Should we perhaps study the matter from the philosophical point of view of art theory?[13]

The latitudinarian view is a potentially awkward one to adopt, because it tends to confound together *style* and *motifs,* which we must keep separate if we are to make sense of the changing attitudes to the past over the last millenium. For there is scarcely an area of post-antique life, from central heating to cosmology, from warfare to art, which is untouched by the example of ancient Greece or Rome. All such influences form the bed-rock, as it were, of the foundations on which Classicism is erected; but we shall not call classical everything that is inspired in some way by the antique because, by concentrating on what unites people rather than on the ways in which they differ, we would arrive at nothing but meaningless generalities. Style and intention, not motif, are therefore the scalpels we shall use in dividing the 'classicists' from the rest. Bernini is a good example in point: he certainly knew as much about the antique as did any of his great forbears (except Palladio); and much of his architecture is an exuberant working out of antique motifs. But the manner in which he does this produces an architecture that is baroque rather than classical in style and effect – a fitting complement to his sources, which were largely from the antique version of the Baroque. Much the same might be said for Caravaggio, whose whole *œuvre* depends on the Renaissance tradition for its sources – but not for its manner. To argue differently is to ignore the startling changes in the painting and sculpture as well and architecture down the centuries.

We must also distinguish between *Classicism* and the *classical tradition* – the former being a state of mind that can exist without reference to any supporting traditions, the latter a conscious assimilation or re-working of characteristics imitated from earlier art and based ultimately on the perceived qualities of antique art. One might say that the classical tradition provides a closely reasoned support for the values of the antique past – the recognised origins of Western civilisation.[14] The very word *tradition* implies more than just conti-

nuity – rather, *tradere* means transmission, handing on; or, in the Roman legal sense, handing something over for safe keeping. Indeed, any survey of the classical tradition in earlier centuries reveals that Classicism is not restricted simply to art, for the adoption of Classicism can carry a whole series of meanings – political, social, ideological and religious; examples illustrating its longevity can therefore be found in such diverse fields as literature,[15] letter forms,[16] coinage[17] and administration. The tradition, indeed, has political as well as social and artistic implications; and it is not going too far to say that the Papacy and the Church have been amongst its most interested supporters since late Antiquity, recognising its value and the support it could lend them. Traditions die only when their usefulness is no longer recognised, and they survive only as long as they can be transmuted. They belong to the realm of ideas: 'What is really a tradition is not the institution, but the belief in its value.'[18]

Indeed, the fact that classical ideals are as clearly evident in literature as in art has led theorists to develop the 'pendulum' theory of artistic sentiment and style, whereby these swing from one extreme to another in supposedly determinable cycles – giving us the oppositions classic and romantic, objective and subjective, rationalist and emotional, reason and imagination, universal and particular, ideal and real. References to the 'neo-classical period' or the 'romantic period' adopt, consciously or subconsciously, the pendulum theory; but we must always bear in mind that not everyone marches to the beat of the same drum, so that it is perfectly possible to have classical productions in a romantic period, and *vice versa.*

Classicism *qua* state of mind is an approach to the arts that emphasises the ideal in form and in content over the everyday; the power of reason over the often misleading emotions – and hence restraint, moderation and self-control; clarity and simplicity – and, usually, understatement over prolixity; measurability as an index of beauty over intuition; and a respect for tradition (hence conservatism and intellectualism). As an example, take Annibale Carracci's *Flight into Egypt,* in the Doria Pamphili Palace Gallery, in Rome (of circa 1604). This evinces no attempt to depict the Flight as it actually took place, for Joseph and the shepherd-boy are dressed in contemporary clothes, while Mary and the boatman wear 'antique' garb. Nor, in spite of the two camels on the left, is the landscape that of Egypt, which the artist could not have known; rather, it depicts the Roman Campagna, with an idealised walled town to the rear, and a version of the

Pantheon therein, together with a waterfall, a river and lake, and a cowherd and shepherd. Because the countryside around Rome has been since ancient times the place for bucolic reverie, Annibale ennobles it into a balanced and dignified setting for the saving of Our Lord from persecution. All the elements of the landscape balance and echo one another, and mark out the importance of the small-scale central figures. Nature is in accord with Man, and it is a tamed nature redolent of antiquity. In formal terms also, the picture is classically balanced, with the swing of the river and of the landscape behind emphasised by the painting's lunette shape. Although some of the elements of the composition go back to the High Renaissance, Annibale's creation is essentially original – an ideal vision in the new genre of historical landscape, inspired by the antique in several ways, but not slavishly chained to it. The same might be said of Michelangelo's Sistine Ceiling, or Lord Burlington's Villa at Chiswick.

From this it is clear that it needs more than the bovine copying of earlier works to make a product classical: the best artists are inspired by classical art and the traditions that grow from it to create what is essentially a new art. Generally, indeed, Classicism is a state of mind and a 'world view'; and style therefore acts as a carrier for ideas – although by the 19th century, it has tended to lose much of its baggage of antique and intellectual associations. Its practitioners believed that the duty of art is to instruct and improve, rather than merely to entertain; and they first sought their models amongst the famous surviving exemplars of the art of Greece and Rome, because their educational ethos put the whole of Antiquity – letters, laws, deeds as well as art – on a pedestal. Along with the study of Greek and Latin, this was much helped by the translation of classical authors into modern languages,[19] as well as by the striving of the moderns to imitate classical vocabulary and style – just as occurred in the visual arts.

The conscious creation of new traditions from the warehouse of classical motifs can be seen in, for example, the development of architecture from the Renaissance. Raphael's Palazzo Vidoni in Rome, of circa 1510, is separated by 150 years from the east facade of the Louvre, of 1667-70, but the family resemblance between the two buildings is clear: a massive basement, coupled columns and entablature, and no attic (that now on Palazzo Vidoni is a later addition). Both use what Summerson would call 'the classical language of architecture' – column, base, capital, podium – but both are recognisably modern buildings, rather than abject (let alone archaeological) imitations of the available antiquities. Indeed,

their designers would not have seen the point of copying the antique; rather, they sought to vie with it in a spirit of admiring competition. For the same reasons Raphael, the painter of *The Borghese Entombment* (derived from an antique sarcophagus relief) would surely have understood David's *Marat Assassiné*, which builds further on Raphael's interpretation and adds an up-to-date meaning.

Since at least the time of Constantine, Classicism has been closely linked with an antique-related political and social vision.[20] So to restrict any survey to art alone is to ignore the diversity of reasons for its potency and longevity, which can be found down the centuries in literature,[21] philosophy,[22] or indeed the very structure of society. Because of this history, the tradition is a set of agreed values, rather than just a conglomeration of styles; and is dependent for its development, nurture and survival on prestigious patronage from rulers or the aristocracy. It is at no time a popular movement, for it often relies on involvement in the linked worlds of scholarship and collecting, as well as education – that is, on the leisure that only money can provide. This is logical, for antique art is also a moneyed or a public art, without working-class elements.

Crucially, the tradition is cumulative rather than consistent. That is, the tradition changes with each generation: so that, for example, 'classical' to the French Ecole des Beaux-Arts in the 19th century meant not only the antique and the Italian Renaissance, but *also* the works of the French Renaissance and 17th century, from Philibert de l'Orme to Francois Mansart and Francois Blondel.[23] This is where academies are important – as a structured, rational support for developing traditions. Were the tradition not cumulative, then it would be a corpse-like, rather than a living and developing phenomenon – a thing always of the past, and *ipso facto* lacking any correspondence to the needs of the present. Indeed, one useful property Classicism was believed to possess was its rationality, in that its main precepts can be expressed as a series of easily explained rules and models: if it could be understood by the mind, extrapolated into a system, subjected to rules and measurements, then it could be taught, and be passed on from generation to generation. Imitation and explication of the accumulated tradition has therefore been the task of many academies – and not just 'art' academies – since their inception in Italy in the 16th century. Hence the development of academies: and just as the tradition itself can be politically oriented, so academies themselves were frequently fuelled by nationalism as well as by artistic theory,[24] often set up by

TEMPLE OF CONCORD, AGRIGENTO, SICILY, c. 430 BC

rulers or scholars for reasons of prestige rather than just training, a point that will later be expanded. Just as any study of academies should comprehend their variety, for they often encompassed all the arts, and not just the 'fine arts', so any account of Classicism should also bear in mind the range of media involved as 'carriers' of the tradition.

### The Classical Tradition: Origins and Importance

This book defines Classicism as a series of reactions to the art and architecture of the Romans and eventually the Greeks, and the associated tradition as something that is both cumulative and changing. Were it to deal with Classicism in all the arts, it would also be necessary to acknowledge the inspiration provided by the ancients to, for example, English literature,[25] as well as to law, rhetoric, or education.[26] There can only be passing reference here, but it must be remembered that for centuries an important measure of the educated man was his knowledge and understanding of the past – that is, of a period which until almost the time of the French Revolution few in Europe believed to have been in any way surpassed. The power – or stranglehold – of the classical past can be seen in, for example, the history of aesthetics.[27]

In any case, given Europe's history and religion, it is scarcely surprising that it was to be the attainments of the greatest Empire ever seen in the West (together with those of its successor, the Byzantine Empire) which fascinated the European successors of Rome. Hence they not only adapted themes and ideas from pagan art to make them acceptable in Christian art, but also retained an interest in their original meanings. In this respect, it is the Middle Ages, the first avid followers of the Antique, which set the 'ground rules', including prestigious foundations like Monte Cassino.[28] The Renaissance merely followed, and invented little new in Christian iconography, for example.[29] And it is this aspect which distinguishes the impact of antique art on alien cultures, such as the Celta[30] – that is, the developing Christian traditions were interested in meanings as well as in forms.

Classicism as a tradition is a conscious attempt to work within such parameters, coupled with respect for past productions. Although it is frequently fashionable to deny the value of tradition, artists and architects can scarcely do without the example of the past; for the majority, the past provides them with sets of ideas, and of useful precedents and pointers, as well as with the security of knowing that they form part of the continuing search by human beings for experience, stability or change. Much more than is frequently realised, art and architecture are based on precedent, and appreciated for reasons connected in some way with the work's connection with the past.

It is not, therefore, surprising that the ancients had their own classical traditions, from which they sought both inspiration and justification for their own work.[31] But it is important to note that copying was not part of the tradition: the Temple of Concord at Agrigento, for example, of about 430BC, is as impressive a survival as the Parthenon, but it held little interest for the Romans, who developed their own variety of temple architecture, only tenuously derived from classical Greek examples. This is why the Southern Italian and Sicilian Greek temples were 'lost' until the 18th century: nobody was interested in them. Rather, it was the Byzantine Empire which, when the Roman Empire in the West was in ruins, acted as an important exemplar (and indeed storeroom) of classical ideas and forms, which were to be of great value to the Italian Renaissance.[32]

Since at least the time of Constantine, and because of the way in which earlier Romans, not to mention Greeks, made use of art in the public arena, Classicism has been closely linked with an antique-related political and social vision, and for this reason has been of varying strength and consistency throughout the medieval and later periods.[33] This interest took various forms. One constant is the re-use of antique spoils in contemporary building, often for sheer convenience,[34] but sometimes as trophies which were perhaps intended to impart a glow of 'millenial civilisation'. This was the case at Venice, a city with a relatively short (and certainly non-antique) history,[35] but which, in other instances, were clearly intended to make some political link. Charlemagne,[36] the Normans[37] and then Frederick II Hohenstaufen[38] and the Papacy are conspicuous in this respect. Revivalism is not limited solely to pagan work as we can see from the concern of both Venice and the Papacy with Early Christian material.[39] Again, the Eastern Empire was a continuing source of classical ideas and motifs during the 'darker' centuries in the West, being often the focus of Western admiration, and sometimes offering authentic re-creations of Hellenistic art as well.[40]

One reason for Classicism's longevity and influence is the rich variety of media in which antique art is to be found. Manuscript illumination and ivories[41] are often especially 'classic' during the Middle Ages, perhaps because smaller antiquities were easily portable, so that their influence could spread widely; while during the later Middle Ages and the Renaissance onwards, the focus is on sculpture and architecture, because of the remains of antique exemplars which became increasingly available during the building booms of the later Middle Ages.[42] Indeed, interest in the classical was fuelled, during the Middle Ages as in later centuries, by continuing and intimate contact with the art of Rome and eventually of Greece. The city of Rome provided a focus of both ideas and forms, and was extensively investigated, and its monuments both imitated and re-used,[43] while their essential symbolism was often preserved as well.[44] But to be classical it was not essential to know work in the city of Rome, for not only could the interested observer in Western Europe usually find Roman remains all around him,[45] but where local antiquities were inadequate or non-existent, both antiquities and their concomitant culture could simply be imported.[46] In other words, the study of the antique (not merely of antique forms of art), while fluctuating in strength, is a constant in Western civilisation up to the 19th century,[47] and if sheer numbers are the criterion, then it is likely that more people in this century have read Homer and Livy than in any other. The crux, of course, is what effect such reading has on the development of their own culture.

Artists who formed part of the classical tradition did so because their clients as well as themselves were part of it – noblemen ordered works from Canova, for example, at least partly because his work rivalled the antiquities they had at home. Indeed, Canova possessed an enormous collection of both antique marbles and terracottas, and it would not be difficult to show that they are essential to his work.[48] The same could be demonstrated for the work of Sir John Soane, Ghiberti or Michelangelo.

All the above indicates that the classical tradition was for hundreds of years an integral element not only in European art and architecture, but also in general culture. Subsequent chapters will trace some aspects of the changing nature of Classicism, and the book will conclude with a discussion of the vital place of Classicism in the ongoing debate about the nature and aims of contemporary architecture.

## Classicism in the Middle Ages and the Renaissance

Led by the example of the Middle Ages, pagan art and architecture were often easily adapted to the needs of Christian art. This happened in the early centuries partly because there were few other exemplars except for the insubstantial productions of the barbarian invaders, but also because of the admiration and amazement with which ancient art was regarded by most barbarians, no less than by indigenous peoples.

BASILICA OF MAXENTIUS, ROME, c. 307-312

Looking today at the Basilica of Maxentius on the Roman Forum, which is in an advanced state of ruin, with few of its porphyry columns left and its cross vaults fallen, it is easy to understand how this and other Roman structures in much better condition scattered over Europe would seem to the Middle Ages the work of a race of supermen, because of their sumptuous sophistication and, in cases like this, their stupendous size.

For centuries, inhabitants of ancient cities lived off the old buildings, using them as a convenient source of ready-made building materials – marble veneer, bricks, columns – or converting existing buildings to new uses. In Syracuse, for example, a Greek temple was converted into the Cathedral, and the original columns are clearly visible down the flanks; in Rome, the Temple of the Divine Romulus, built in about 309 AD, became in the sixth century the vestibule of the church of SS Cosmas & Damian, the church proper using part of the structure of Vespasian's Forum of Peace. In Early Christian times, new churches were often constructed after the manner of Roman civic basilicas, in new locations but using available antique remains. In addition, small pieces of antique art were also re-used – capitals made good holy water stoups or wellheads when hollowed out; sarcophagi, espe-

cially sculpted ones, and also cinerary urns were highly prized, and were transported great distances; small ivory panels, some of them in tablet form as diptychs, frequently found their way into church treasuries; antique coins were collected and copied. Most works in precious metals suffered the inevitable fate, however.

The result of such interest in the antique, sometimes for reasons of prestige, sometimes to make a political or aesthetic point, was that the Middle Ages surrounded itself with the works of Antiquity whenever possible.

What is more, they so steeped themselves in their qualities that it was natural for many of their own artistic productions, from manuscripts to churches, to follow an antique, if not strictly a classical, manner. To think of the Renaissance as merely the rebirth of interest in the antique is therefore to miss the point that the Middle Ages itself saw a whole series of renascences[49] without which the more profound and long-lasting Italian Renaissance could not have been possible.[50] The Renaissance of the 12th century was particularly important because it was Europe-wide. In Sicily, the mid-12th-century Paschal Candlestick in the Palatine Chapel, Palermo, shows a re-use both of classical dress and of the acanthus, well-known from antique Corinthian capitals.

RAPHAEL, VATICAN LOGGIA, ROME

So prestigious was the aura provided by links with Roman antiquity that, just as the once-barbarian invaders had adopted and imitated it, so likewise did other invaders: the Arabs, a nomadic desert people with no architectural traditions of their own, learned much from Roman and Byzantine art and architecture, with the result that many of the sources of Islamic art are to be found in the Mediterranean past. As well as re-using actual monuments, they imitated them as well. At Madinet al Zahra (Cordoba, Spain), for example, the calif Abderrahman II (912-61) built a sumptuous palace in marble and mosaic which rivalled Byzantine productions, and using adapted classical motifs: a column base, decorated with basket work and bas-relief, is obviously inspired by Roman productions, perhaps local ones.

If the Renaissance differed in anything from the previous centuries, it was in the methodical and enthusiastic way in which antiquity was studied, rather than just plundered or refurbished, as had been generally the case. Antique art theory and aesthetics were studied, and whole courts devoted themselves to the study and expression of the antique in philosophy, theatre, history and rhetoric, as well as law and the visual arts. Following the surge of population after about 1100AD, and in spite of the toll taken by the Black Death, Europe began to enjoy a prosperity unknown since Roman times. Its first tokens are the great Romanesque and Gothic churches, the antique sources of the former being clear, those of the latter less so.[51] There was an upsurge of building, and of associated artistic patronage, generally but not exclusively driven by an interest in classical ideas and forms. Because so much of the comparative evidence has subsequently been lost, it is only from the clues provided by recent research that we know that the range of antiquities studied was very wide indeed: frescoes were used as models for paintings;[52] but small antiquities such as pottery lamps, and coins and medals from as far away as Asia Minor, also served Renaissance artists.

One important feature of Renaissance art is the thirst for knowledge of the antique as a means of developing new styles. Renaissance scholars and artists were certainly interested in antiquity *per se* but their enthusiasm for its art was also helped (and perhaps partly provoked?) by their equally strong concern for nature and naturalism,[53] the latter being one of the features of antique sculpture which much amazed the Middle Ages. The aim was always to use nature together with the antique as a device for constructing the ideal, and never in order to conjure up a 'realistic' version of life: the depiction of those aspects of ordinary life so popular in 19th-

RAPHAEL, STUDY OF THE THREE GRACES

century art were spurned by the Renaissance. The involvement with the antique as a motor for the development of new classicising styles is often easiest to see in sculpture, where many ancient examples existed above ground or were easily retrieved by deliberate exploratory digging, or found by chance in the course of agricultural or building work.[54]

In many Renaissance works, antique sculptural exemplars serve as much for paintings as they do for sculptures. In most cases their general parentage is clearly proclaimed not hidden, because the new works are imitations not copies; and, as is always the case with traditions, the cognoscenti would be expected both to recognise the source and to admire what the artist had done with it. For this reason, Renaissance art does not – any more than is the case with architecture – stand in a one-to-one relationship with the antique, and identifiable straight copies are rare.[55]

The works of Raphael, arguably the most influential painter in the history of Western art, also derive their motifs from antique sculpture and architecture,[56] as well as from the Early Christian tradition. He probably knew ancient fresco *ensembles,* now lost, as his marvellous illusionistic bays in the Vatican Logge suggest.[57]

## Classicism in Medieval and Renaissance Architecture

The architectural and sculptural opportunities of the triumphal arch provide another good example of the effects of thoughtful imitation. This was one of the forms which could be used exactly as it was in Antiquity, for triumphal processions. Antique arches in stone or marble are still to be found all over the territory of the Roman Empire, although many have been destroyed. In Rome, for example, were several antique examples, one of the most richly decorated, in both sculptures and marbles, being the Arch of Constantine. Their meaning was plain, and hence there are plenty of examples of imitation in the Renaissance and later. These were usually temporary structures of wood and canvas used for pageants. But the format was also suitable for re-modelling to provide imposing entrances to buildings, and as such it has never ceased to be popular. The triumphal arch to the Castel Nuovo in Naples, honouring Alfonso V who conquered the city in 1442, takes the antique motif and adapts it: the Castel Nuovo is tall, its entrance narrow, so the proportions are adjusted; the usual winged victories over the main arch are replaced by a coat of arms; Alfonso appears as *triumphator* on the second storey in a frieze distantly reminiscent of those under Trajan's Arch; allegorical statues top another arch on the next storey,

MICHELANGELO, CAMPIDOGLIO, CAPITALINE MUSEUM, ROME, 1537-61

this time with victories, and this is capped by a pediment bearing reclining river gods holding cornucopia, denoting plenty. Intricate detailing is saved for the podium at eye level, which sports classical putti, an oak leaf 'torus' denoting victory, and classicising profile heads crowned with diadems.

Because we live in an age where there is a profligate use of styles, meaning tends to get devalued, so that we are inclined to forget the kinds of messages that architecture once carried. Classical architecture is much more than a language: rather, it represents a whole nexus of power and even domination. Thus Fraser, noting the use of the Doric Order of architecture in Spanish America, notes that it 'suggests both the great antiquity as well as the solid foundations of the conquerors' religion. The new order is marked by the return to a set of architectural fundamentals, which have their roots in a literate tradition.'[58] To take a broader view, with hindsight, it is also the case that 'the Renaissance revival of classical architecture by an educated elite began the estrangement of architecture from the popular consciousness'[59] – an estrangement with, arguably, dire consequences for the health and acceptance of architecture in our century.

Elitism – the coded and easily adaptable language of a ruling class – is but one reason for the popularity of classical architecture. Another is that ancient principles could be seen and applied in architecture more easily than in painting or even sculpture, and for this reason the tradition is much clearer, although not continuous, in architecture than in the other arts.[60] This is because many remains of ancient architecture survived throughout the Middle Ages in recognisable condition. The various medieval imitations in France, Spain and Germany, as well as in Italy, demonstrated that a new architecture could be erected according to the perceived principles of the old.[61] Italy became the seat of the Renaissance and hence the leading light of Classicism at least partly because her soil was so rich in imitable antiquities, but also because it was the Italians who developed a coherent theory of architecture.[62]

The development of a suitable church architecture was not a problem. The majority of Renaissance churches are a variation on the pagan basilica, first developed for worship in Early Christian times, and then re-worked by Alberti under the inspiration of antique exemplars,[63] as may be seen in the magnificent triumphal arch, together with its austere barrel vaulting, which he gives to his church of S Andrea at Mantua, of 1470. However, an indication of the attempt to blend antique forms with Christian ideals is that the Renaissance

L B ALBERTI, SANTA MARIA NOVELLA, FLORENCE, c. 1456-70

was passionately interested in building centrally-planned churches. Inspired by a mixture of pagan tombs and temples and Christian baptistries and usually capped by a dome, they expressed the perfection of God as well as being a beautiful shape, whether round (or hexagonal or octagonal) or square. The great model was the Pantheon in Rome, whose coffered semi-circular dome spanned nearly 44 metres. Bramante tried to use it for his new St Peter's, but was unable to support a similarly single-skinned dome. Central-plan churches which did get built include S Maria della Consolazione at Todi (1508ff), and Antonio da Sangallo the Elder's Madonna di San Biagio, at Montepulciano (1518-29), a Greek cross design with rectangular arms, and the orders correctly displayed on the one campanile which was completed, after the model of the Colosseum. But the most famous of all was Bramante's Tempietto in San Pietro in Montorio, perhaps begun in 1502 – a martyrium on the supposed site of Peter's death, and derived from Roman tombs and from temples like the Temple of Vesta at Tivoli (although this has a Corinthian peristyle, unlike the austerely chaste Doric used by Bramante). After the prominence given much more in their theory than in their practice by the Renaissance to the central plan, such buildings – whether churches or secular structures – have exercised great influence ever since. Bernini's Sant'Andrea al Quirinale, Rome, and the Catholic cathedral in Liverpool, are but two examples of the popularity of this configuration.

Public architecture also used antique examples, but much more adaptation was necessary, as in Michelangelo's palace facades for the Capitoline Hill in Rome, completed after his death. As with his New Sacristy at San Lorenzo, Florence (1521-34), and his contribution to St Peter's, he uses a giant order of pilasters to tie two storeys together into a balanced unity. The device is derived from Roman triumphal arches, and it was henceforth very popular: Giulio Romano uses it for the Palazzo Te at Mantua (1525-35) and, placed on a high podium, it becomes a commonplace of palace architecture, not only for Palladio, but also for Bernini, as in his Palazzo Odescalchi in Rome (1664ff).

Domestic architecture was a problem, for there was no truly reliable knowledge of Roman town-houses or villas until the 18th century. Andrea Palladio, however, was undeterred. He assiduously drew antique remains, developed designs for both houses and villas which he not only publicised in his well-illustrated *Quattro libri dell'architettura* of 1570, but legitimised, as it were, in his illustrations to Daniele Barbaro's 1556 edition of Vitruvius, the only architectural text to survive from Antiquity. His plans are symmetrical, and his designs rich and splendid: he demonstrated how to incorporate antique temple fronts into domestic architecture. Best known is the Villa Capra (or Rotunda) outside Vicenza, begun in 1552, which places four pillared porticos on each side of the square block, and caps the structure with a central dome, giving the whole a festive appearance that looked convincingly classical but which, of course, is like no antique villa ever built, since antique houses looked inwards, not outwards). Similar is the Villa Trissino at Melodo, with its colonnades marching up the hill, the structure crowned by a temple front and a dome. In fact villas like this, with their attention to the lie of the land, reveal Palladio's study of antique temple complexes, such as the Temple of Fortuna Primigenia at Palestrina.[64]

Such adaptations of ancient ideas to modern needs are veritable *tours de force* – sophisticated and learned, but also exuberant and often playful. They not only made Palladio's fortune, but ensured that he would be the most influential of all architects.[65] And even if the 18th century was to find him too exuberant, and to tone down his manner, an index of his influence can be seen by visiting the site of several of his own creations – namely the River Brenta from Vicenza toward Venice – and observing the many later villas that are still recognisable variants of the Palladian manner. The spread of his fame can be gauged by a tour of the Eastern States of the USA or, indeed, by visiting 18th-century English or Scottish country houses such as Robert Adam's Kedleston Hall.

Palladio's designs are no more 'archaeological' or 'correct' than those of Brunelleschi, Alberti or Michelangelo. But this was not the intention. Rather, Renaissance architecture and its heritage are variations inspired by antique themes, and adapted for modern needs. The aim was not to re-create antique forms, but to create new buildings which might incorporate antique ideas – an aim which has served as the main measure of European taste from the virtual invention of Renaissance architecture by Brunelleschi at the beginning of the 15th century, until the beginning of the Baroque[66] and has never really died out, influencing town planning and indeed the very ethos of civilised life.[67] The Villa Albani, for example, begun in 1743 and enhanced from 1775 following the advice of Winckelmann by a splendid collection of antiquities is an 18th-century classical ensemble – not just of architecture, but of statues and paintings as well.[68] The general effect sought by Winckelmann (a connoisseur of the antique and Cardinal Alessandro Albani's librarian, but not an architect), is one with which the owner of Villa Trissino or of Kedleston Hall would have felt at home; while the Getty Museum at Malibu, California, is a careful reproduction of a Pompeian villa, designed to complement classical collections in exactly the same way.[69] Such structures enhance the importance of the art works they contain because they provide an appropriate setting – a fashion which will be taken over as the format for public museums.

If Classicism in painting and sculpture could spread because it was rational and hence teachable, so could it also in architecture, where printed treatises often incorporating antique designs were produced in the vernacular languages, so that they could be understood by builders and well as by gentleman-scholars. Vitruvius and Palladio were quickly taken up abroad, especially in France and England, French architecture in the 16th century developing almost exclusively under the influence of Italian ideas and Italian architects. At Chambord, Renaissance motifs are simply stuck onto a medieval chateau. For Ancy le Franc, however, begun in 1546, Sebastiano Serlio, the author of *L'Architettura* (6 vols, 1537-51), imported a sober and simple classical style: this, together with Philibert de l'Orme's work at Anet (and *his* book, the *Architecture*, of 1567), launched a specifically French classical style, which was to be further developed by Salomon de Brosse, Lescot, and the great architects of the following century such as Jacques Lemercier and Francois Mansart. In England, if the adoption of Italian ideas was slower, it was eventually equally important, with the work of Inigo Jones and Lord Burlington. Although both France and England (and, indeed, the rest of Western Europe) were to develop their own particular varieties of Classicism, architecture as a carrier of ideas is particularly significant. This is not only because of its cost, but also because it provides the showcase within which the other arts can most gloriously be

## The 17th Century

Problems of the definition of Classicism are particularly acute for the 17th century which, in Italy and parts of the North, is often called the *Age of Baroque,* but which, in France, is generally called the *Age of Classicism.* During the previous century, the Renaissance manner, with its varieties of Classicism, had gradually spread over Europe, taken by Italian artists and architects to eager princes and monarchs, studied in Italy by foreigners, both artists and visitors on educational tours, and confirmed by the dissemination of art works ancient and modern, of reproductive prints both singly and by the volume, and of illustrated text-books. Italian art and architecture retained the initiative for at least the first half of the 17th century, but its influence declined somewhat as Northern cultures developed their own, nationally coloured versions of the Renaissance manner.

Baroque, the exuberant and emotional union of the arts, with its illusionism and colour, is the style predominant in Rome during the maturity of Bernini, who contributed greatly to its development. It is essentially a Catholic art and, although retaining an admixture of classical forms, for this very reason it does not travel well either to the Protestant countries of the North, or to France, with its 'separatist' version of Catholicism and its strongly developing Classicism. Classicism, however, could not fail to be influenced by the vigour of the Baroque, any more than politicians could fail to realise that its colour and power, erstwhile servants of religion, could so easily be turned to the service of the State. A modified Baroque, sometimes known as Baroque Classicism, found its fortune in the autocratic monarchies of France and even Britain, where the original excesses were tamed, and local colouring added. In this way Baroque (which of course was also inspired by antique art and architecture, especially that of Hellenism) helped modify and re-invigorate Classicism, making it richer and more exuberant, and the better suited to the expression of political absolutism.

In France, Classicism was developed as a new style with French features, underpinned by the justificatory theorising offered by newly founded academies. Proof of the development of a truly French manner is seen in the work of Nicholas Poussin who, although residing almost permanently in Italy, produced paintings on classical subjects in a severe, restrained and thoughtful manner which was to be in French Classicism the touchstone for artists as diverse as David, Ingres and Cézanne. In Paris and provincial cities, not to mention on large estates, public buildings, churches and châteaux were built whose parentage in Italian Renaissance architecture is certainly traceable, but whose style is *new*. The manner is exemplified by the east façade of the Louvre, a long colonnade erected by Perrault (with the aid of LeBrun and Le Vau) from 1667, which marks the decisive rejection of the designs for the same building solicited from Bernini, and hence of the full Italian Baroque style. With the east façade of the Louvre, one might say that French architecture came of age, just as the organisation and control of all the arts in France came of age with the establishment of a wide range of royally supported academies.

N POUSSIN, *THE NURTURE OF JUPITER*, OIL ON CANVAS, c.1635, 96.2 X 119.6 CM

In Britain, where academies only came much later, Inigo Jones created almost single-handed a classical style based on Italian models, which is still to be seen in his Italianate Queen's House at Greenwich, of the 1630s. This largely inspired the Palladian revival of Lord Burlington in the early 18th century, and both he and Burlington laid the groundwork for the subsequent explosion of classicising country houses. In painting and sculpture, however, there was nobody to equal Poussin in either prestige or influence; and it was not until Sir Joshua Reynolds' *Discourses* – delivered between 1769 and 1790 to the Royal Academy, founded in 1768 – that a deliberate attempt was made to set up a British school of history painting in the continental manner – the more intellectual version of Classicism, for which Richard Wilson developed the landscape arm from the later 1740s.

The contribution of the 17th century to Classicism meant, taking the broad view, its liberation from the confines of the Italian peninsula, which had made the running in classicising art and architecture for well over two hundred years, and its launch as a European language of expression, easily adaptable to local circumstances. In this it was indeed helped by the Baroque which, as well as demonstrating other sources for architects (particularly Hellenistic work), showed painters and sculptors how the dried-out conventions of Mannerism could be side-stepped, and High Renaissance Classicism given a more sensuous and lively aspect.

## The 18th Century: History and Neo-Classicism

A constant theme of Classicism is the discovery and treament of sources. The Middle Ages generally used nearby ruins as models, often removing from them for re-use not only basic building materials, but also fine marbles and even art works. Renaissance architects travelled more widely, but their horizons were usually restricted to material to be found in Italy, Provence and Dalmatia. The 17th century began to travel much more widely, with scholars, artists, architects and draftsmen visiting and reporting on monuments in Greece and Egypt, Asia Minor and Syria. But it was in the 18th century when such 'research travel' became a passion, and a methodical one at that. In Britain, for example, the Society of Dilettanti, founded in 1734, paid for visits and the ensuing publications of finds and travels. Objects were also brought back to be used as models, as well as for prestigious display.[70]
This broadening of sources affected the nature of Classicism. In architecture, more emphasis came to be placed on accuracy of drawing, and hence on the notion of correct/incorrect, to a

degree which would certainly have puzzled Brunelleschi or Palladio. A larger range of sources fitted a more style-conscious and sophisticated market, and a history-conscious one at that. Greek architecture made its appearance in a tradition hitherto dominated by the products of the Roman Empire. Concern with accuracy in its turn induced an interest in purity, and with it the realisation that the Romans themselves had frequently been 'incorrect'. Put together with the new interest in Greece, this placed Greek architecture (theoretically at least) to the forefront, as both pure and simple – whereas Roman productions were seen as florid and flawed. The same general trends are apparent in painting and sculpture. The trickle of disinterred and imported antiquities became a flood, its range much broader than hitherto. Archaic Greek art, and Greek painting on vases, began to be appreciated. And Renaissance traditions, once viewed as austere in comparison with the Baroque, were now perceived as over-complicated. In two-dimensional arts, the search for simplicity and purity took its most extreme form in a return to linearity, partly inspired by antique vase painting.

In all, the 18th century saw a systematisation of knowledge, with a surge in the natural sciences and in discoveries about the world and mankind, and a veritable boom in publishing. This happened not just in the visual arts, but in many fields of scholarship: it is, after all, the age of the Enlightenment, of the French *Encyclopédie* and its many more specialised surveys and compendia in all languages. The study of history, and the writing of history, became a discipline which could apparently proceed according to 'scientific' principles, and yield real knowledge – not just whimsical opinions – about the past. In the visual arts, the most conspicuous outcome of this passionate interest in the past was the foundation of museums and galleries, usually clothed in the glory of classical architecture,[71] and intended until at least the French Revolution to contain examples of classical and classicising art.

Since the Middle Ages, connoisseurs have sought to make collections of antique and contemporary art, and these may sometimes have been formed for aesthetic enjoyment alone, many were put together for reasons of political and social prestige. Often open for study by artists (such as the famous if mysterious 'sculpture garden' of Lorenzo de'Medici), they formed an essential complement to the intellectual interests of that class of individuals – 'connoisseurs', 'curieux' – who would today be called 'opinion formers', and whose interest in the ancient world extended to literature, history and phi-

losophy as well as art. Whereas most early collections were in Italy, by the 16th century there were impressive ones in Germany, and by the next century in France and Britain as well. The institution of the Grand Tour, which allowed the British aristocracy and gentry to complete their education at the fountainhead of Classicism, namely Italy, also offered the opportunity for the purchase of ever-increasing quantities of works of art; so that, by 1800, we can truly speak of an *international* interest in collecting.[72] Prints – the picture-postcards of the day – offered memories of the works to admire, as in Muller's print after Pannini's painting of *The Ruins of Ancient Rome,* which includes the Pantheon, the Belvedere Torso, the Column of Marcus Aurelius and the Temple of the Sibyl from Tivoli, all grouped together into an ideal view.

Quatremère de Quincy, a prominent writer about matters artistic, and influential in the French system of academies, believed that museums are indeed the death of art. This might seem strange after the nearly two hundred years during which the concept of the museum and its sister, the art gallery, had grown from strength to strength, but it neatly makes the distinction between the living art which takes its natural part in even a changing society, and the dead art which is enshrined for educational and academic purposes in a temple-like storehouse. In this opinion, Quatrèmere was against the tide of his time, although not completely alone;[73] and his opinion was echoed later, as by the critic Théophile Thore: 'Museums are only the cemeteries of art, catacombs in which are arranged, in sepulchral promiscuity, the remains of what was once alive'.[74] Other scholars, such as Aloys Hirt[75] saw museums more optimistically as the ideal organisms by which contemporary art might be rejuvenated through a study of the classical past. This is an opinion which permeates the 19th century, but the consequences of which were most unfortunate, entailing the nexus *modern = new,* but *classical = dead = museum,* as Quatremère had so clearly and accurately foreseen.

What is more, the very prestige of the antique was under attack, and its place in the fabric of artistic production was being reassessed. Hegel, for example, while acknowledging the beauty of the antique, believed that its time was past; and that modern, Romantic and Christian art necessarily superseded it:

When romantic art takes the Christian unity of the divine and human for its content, it abandons altogether the ideal of reciprocal adequacy of content and form at-

JOHANN SEBASTIAN MULLER, AFTER G P PANNINI, *RUINS OF ANCIENT ROME*

tained by classical art. And in its efforts to free itself from the immediately sensuous as such . . . romantic art becomes indeed the transcendence of art itself.[76]

Thus museums were, at the best, a two-edged sword: they preserved ever-increasing quantities of classical antiquities, while art galleries were to do the same for paintings and sculptures from later ages. But neither was exclusively classical in their contents, so that the products of the Middle Ages, and indeed of non-European cultures, were soon to occupy the same qualitative pedestal as those of Antiquity, even if they never received an equivalent amount of attention. Even assuming, therefore, that contemporary artists wished to be 're-juvenated' by classical art, the museum as it developed in the first half of the 19th century was very different from the typical country house collection on which it was usually based, as were the educational horizons of many of the people who visited it. It may not be too cynical to suggest that the whole institution was an attempt to sanctify an upper-class educational and cultural ethos as a target at which inferior classes, in that century of self-improvement, might aim their attention.

If these strictures did not on their own spell sufficient difficulties for the position of museums within a rapidly changing culture, they were helped along by an increasingly dog-matic – because historical and even archaeological – attitude to the past. That is, in the course of the 18th century the very *perception* of Classicism changed from a freely inventive and 'inspirational' approach to the art of Rome, to a more dogmatic one. This is *Neo-Classicism*, founded partly on a reaction to the excesses of the Baroque, and partly on the new scholarship of history – as opposed to mere antiquarianism[77] – which was responsible for a more systematic approach to the past. For the visual arts and architecture, it was the increased pace of archaeology, provoked from the mid-century by spectacular finds at Pompeii and Herculaneum, which provided a much wider range of possible models, from hairpins and tripods to frescoes. Easier travel into the Eastern Mediterranean brought not only the Elgin Marbles to Britain, but whole shiploads of spoils from the archaic and classical periods to populate the new museums of Europe.[78] Hence the art and architecture of Greece, which had hitherto with few exceptions been little noticed by Europeans, could now compete with the products of Rome, to the latter's detriment in esteem, if not in sheer quantity of building or artefact output. Some of its most prestigious sculptures and vases (ie paintings) were in Europe; and its architecture was available to students through measured drawings as well as views. The

Greek language, increasingly better known in Europe since the Renaissance, although never as common as Latin, was now widely taught in schools and universities. Even the history of art (a subject almost invented by Ghiberti and Vasari), beginning with the writings of Winckelmann, was to chart and to rationalise the rise of Greek and the consequent fall of Roman art.

Such systematisation was underpinned by a much-increased level of publication. And if some tend to blame Mannerism's 'mistakes in classical grammar' on the over-use of text-books without sight of the exemplars themselves, it was by the early 19th century quite possible for those intent on building to have in their libraries well-illustrated volumes covering the great majority of structures antique and modern. It should be remembered that, for the Society of Dilettanti, seeing antiquities was essential: from 1764, one of their rules read: 'That no Person can be proposed to be admitted to this Society who cannot bring sufficient proof of his having been in Italy, or upon some other Classic Ground out of the King's Dominions and at his own request'.[79] This is radically different from its perhaps essential adjunct, but no more than an adjunct for all that – namely reading books on the matter. The development of the public museum during the 19th century, together with the decline of enterprise collecting by individuals, changed the very values of Classicism. These had previously been an essential complement to a universally accepted system of education, in that everyone had agreed on the importance of the classical and classicising past for contemporary life. For the 19th century, however, the scale of values was much broader, and Classicism, hitherto supreme, had now to struggle for survival against the competing claims of other value systems.

## Classicism in Painting and Sculpture: 18th and 19th Centuries

We have already seen the new directions introduced into the study of Classicism by the development of museums, and have adduced some reasons for these. There are others: in the 18th and 19th centuries, art changed mainly because the society supporting and feeding it changed more radically and in a shorter time than it had ever done before. There were increased literacy and publication rates for books and periodicals; better communications; a powerful and apparently unstoppable industry-based prosperity; an enlarged bourgeoisie and powerful professions, together with the decline of the aristocracy; a much enlarged artistic community; the invention of photography, and the consequent questioning of the aims of art – all these were factors in change, and especially in its international nature. Similar ideas and styles in all the arts can be found from Sweden to Germany and England to Italy. From the 18th century, such radical changes in society[80] spelled a different outlook on the supposedly eternal values espoused by the classical tradition, for other equally valid systems were introduced to compete with it; 19th-century patronage was largely bourgeois, and little interested in the classical past, especially since Renaissance traditions were also under attack from a plethora of new styles and sources,[81] as can clearly be seen from the changing – indeed, broadening – aesthetic perceptions of the period.[82]

Change can itself provoke turmoil, in art as in the social structure; and the 18th and 19th centuries are for this reason a confusing period, with no one clear style or approach. Thanks to an increased interest in the past, eclecticism came into vogue, and so several were espoused at the same time. The French Revolution, for example, saw the encouragement of neo-classical and of romantic styles. Rome and indeed Italy, the fountainhead of Classicism for the Renaissance, now inspired Romantic artists as well as classicising ones.[83] the Victorians, deeply interested in romantic medievalism, also appreciated classical themes.[84] Classicism and the myths of traditional history painting were also brought into play in the 19th century to justify current ideologies about the different natures and hence importance, of men and women – pictorial ideograms, suggests Kestner,[85] with profound political and social implications. In a sense, indeed, the archaeological interests of the 19th century (fuelled in part by the opening up of Greece and, in the mid-century, by the development of the whole gamut of tourism) created an historicising, archaeological version of Classicism that is frigid rather than alive – so that scholarship (and its child historicism) helped to alter radically the complexion of Classicism.[86]

This expansion of focus from the classic lands to the whole Mediterranean basin and, indeed, further afield, takes place against a background of enlarged geographical horizons – the British in India, the French in Egypt and North Africa, the Dutch in the Far East, and many European nations in Africa south of the Sahara. New geographical horizons are accompanied by broadened intellectual ones, in the context of which Antiquity is seen as but one of a range of possible beacons to follow. Key texts are Montesquieu's *L'esprit des lois* of 1748 and, in art, the dispute in 1765/6 between Diderot and Falconet on the respect to be accorded the Ancients[87] itself but a particular focus of the long-running and multi-discipline *Querelle des Anciens et des Moderness*.[88] Its proponents are the spiritual ancestors of those who, rejecting classical conventions, sought others 'which enlarged the expressive potentials of modern art. These were the productions of the various archaic, non-European, and so-called primitive cultures which had previously been considered tentative, exotic or inept by the standards of Graeco-Roman aesthetica.'[89]

Perhaps most seriously, given its perennially important place in the classical tradition, the influence of Rome falls before the supposed cultural superiority of Greece[90] – and this in the decades before the Greek Wars. Hence the *Roman* classical tradition is devalued, partly by an interest in the linearity and 'chastity' of Greek vase painting, which produced a short-lived but international style, the *tabula rasa* of Rosenblum, most notably in the work of Flaxman[91] and of Canova. The latter's *Achilles gives Briseis to the Heralds* takes inspiration from famous statues such as the *Apollo Belvedere* as well as from vases. However, there are no solid foundations upon which immediately to replace Roman with Greek. The result is not so much a vacuum, as a devaluation of the whole tradition: Greece now becomes one of a whole series of possible styles or fashions, but does *not* replace Rome as a stable tradition. Not that this prevents the development of a Greek ideal during the 19th century, firmly welded to Western consciousness by education, with sensitive souls in both the 19th century and the 20th decrying the 'brutal insensitivity' of the public, and calling again for a cultured *elite* after the model of Athens or Florence – so that one wonders whether 'to be civilised' *still* demands a concern for Greece and Rome.[92] One might argue, perhaps, that the whole swing from interest in Rome, which had been part of the European heritage since early medieval times, to the apparently purer, more original art of Greece (which is scarcely influential except via the Romans themselves) is the direct result not of love or passion for the art of the past, but part of an intellectual movement comprehending archaeology and literature. Correctness becomes a virtue, not just a style, and many architects are themselves archaeologists, such as Leo von Klenze.[93] Von Klenze's own architecture is intimately connected with his archaeology, the former being the outcome of the latter.[94] Based on extensive travel, it is therefore *not* artificial, any more than it is a simplistic imitation of the antique.

Other forces were also at work from the middle of the 18th century. Denis Diderot (1713-84), writer of plays, co-com-piler of the great *Encyclopédie* (1751ff) and art critic, encouraged the painter Greuze to develop narrative bourgeois – not aristocratic – painting, because he considered bourgeois life a worthy subject for art, and art a good vehicle for imparting true morality. Henceforth, 'good' painting did not have to be on antique or noble themes, the preserve of lords and princes: it could deal with ordinary, everyday life. There is no need to expand on the development of these ideas in the 19th century, except to underline that they affected attitudes to Classicism because classical motifs and style were now to be transposed to serve themes lately perceived as unworthy of attention. The change can be understood by comparing Riccio's *Death Scene* in the Louvre (based on antique sarcophagus reliefs) with Daniel Chodowiecki's print of the *Farewell of Calas to his Family*, of 1768. Riccio is using an antique motif called the *conclamatio*, where the family is called together to witness the last moments of the dying person. The essentials of the scene are a couch, suitably draped, and with a grief-stricken figure at its foot, the family around, and an atmosphere of austere nobility. Chodoweicki transforms antique heroism into a contemporary context, with this victim of intolerance about to be taken away to die. Is this, then, a perversion of the classical tradition – of a motif which survives intact in, for example, David's *Socrates taking the Hemlock* of 1787? In one sense, the Renaissance had shown the way, by fitting such scenes to their own purposes, whether bourgeois or noble, as in Verrocchio's relief of the *Death of the wife of Giovanni Tornabuoni* in the Bargello, Florence; but on the other, the Renaissance work maintains a rarified nobility of tone, whereas Chodowiecki's piece (and many of Greuze's would-be adaptations of noble themes) prefers anecdote to simplicity, and description to idealism. The classical motifs are still there, in a sense – the fainting wife in a chair at the foot of the box on which he sits, the grieving family. But this is now a farewell, *not* a true death scene, and is sentimental rather than noble.

The French Revolution might have helped change the nature of official art but, with its antique-based philosophy it did not lessen the need for it, and Antiquity became a veritable cult,[95] confirmed and enlarged by Napoleon as Consul and then as Emperor. However, after Napoleon it was the bourgeois approach typified by Greuze, with unidealised and sometimes realistic scenes of everyday modern life, which won the day. In the 19th century, then, following such trends, history painting was to decline in importance, and genre painting (even historical genre painting) to take its place.[96]

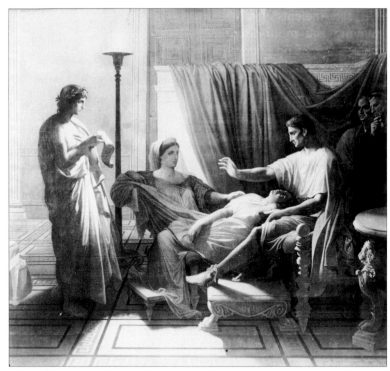

J-A-D INGRES, *VIRGIL READING THE AENEID TO AUGUSTUS*, 1812, OIL ON CANVAS

The system of official patronage broke down, and bourgeois tastes took over. Classicism, for so long linked to the official point of view, or the rarified ideals of cognoscenti, could not easily adapt to this radical, if prolonged, change in taste.

If in Britain Classicism had overtones of the establishment, in France the situation was much more complex, because of the pervasiveness of Romanticism: for that century, what *exactly* was classical, and what romantic? The work of the painter Ingres, himself the earnest champion of Classicism against what he saw as the devilry of Delacroix, is itself a good example of this eclecticism. For although often presented as a died-in-the-wool classicist, there is enough of the medievalist and indeed the realist about Ingres to demonstrate the fragility, in a 19th-century context, of the once-valid stylistic divisions.[97] For Ingres, it is the subject that dictates the style: he can produce antiquarianism as good as that of Vien or David, as in his *Virgil reading the Aeneid to Augustus* (Toulouse, 1812); Raphael revised by Poussin, so to speak, as in his *Christ giving the Keys to Peter* (Montauban 1820), and any number of part-Mannerist, part-'realistic' portraits. Nevertheless, it was Ingres who, with Poussin, inspired the Classicism of that of his great and influential successor, Puvis de Chavannes.[98]

What is more, in the course of the 19th century the nature of academies changes profoundly, as does the educational ethos; and Classicism, the 'carrier' of academic art and the ornament of and justification for traditional educational values, suffers as a result. There are reasons to believe, with Brendel, that academic teaching becomes narrower as time goes on, so that 19th-century artists are left with no more than the husk of a tradition: 'In the practice of the schools the meaning of this term, "classical", thereby tended to become rather narrowly defined: it came to mean little more than a faithful adherence to this handful of generally recommended models and the principles thought to be incorporated in them'[99]

Frequently, the adulation of the antique was further formalised because it proceeded by way of copies, which tended further to formalise and perhaps deaden instruction.[100] We might believe that Neo-Classicism – the conscious imitation of the antique, especially that of recent archaeological discoveries in the 18th and 19th centuries – is a cause of this process.[101] Thus the continuation – however shaky it may now appear to have been – of the academic tradition also ensured the continuance of the imitation of the antique, noticeably in French sculpture, where artists like Carpeaux, Bourdelle,

J-L DAVID, *THE DEATH OF SOCRATES*, 1787, OIL ON CANVAS, 128 X 192.5 CM

Barye and Maillol (to cite only the best known) produced many works which are sometimes quotations, sometimes variations, on antique sources. Such works represent an 'advance' over those of the previous century only in their wider range of sources, such as classical and pre-classical Greek,[102] following on the lead of the Danish sculptor Thorvaldsen.[103]

Generally, however, classical styles in the 19th century became almost completely detached from their original context and purpose, at least partly as a result of the convenience of study in museums and galleries; and from this came their acceptance by the increasingly industrialised world as decoration. Industrialisation itself demanded either an acceptance of new techniques, or retrenchment in the old manner. But the usual way out was by the multiplication of traditional forms – capitals, statues, chimneypots – using semi-industrial techniques. The newly-expanding middle classes could afford some version of the Venus de Milo on the mantlepiece, or a classical colonnade framing the front door. What is startling about the 19th century, however, is the lack of interest on the part of architects in machine-age techniques, except for 'low' projects such as industrial and commercial buildings, so that the opportunity to 'bring Classicism up to date' by develop-ing a new vocabulary to suit new materials was lost. Argua-bly, this was to have a profound effect on the subsequent career of classicising architecture, for the gulf was not to be bridged. As Mumford writes of Jefferson's classicality: 'What Jefferson did not realise . . . is that two kinds of universal language were now being spoken in architecture: a dead language, that of the classics, and a live language, that of the machine.'[104]

Examples of this dichotomy between tradition and ma-chine are legion, from classical chimney-pots to printing presses. *The High Pressure Steam Engine* (by Ernst Alban, 1839) in the Deutsches Museum in Munich is a good ex-ample, with the structure supported on four (miniature, of course) baseless, cannellated columns, and with correct en-tablature, the whole in steel. The vocabulary is there, but does its use make the product classical? Surely not, because there is no inner logic, no rationale, behind its employment.

Taking the broad view of 19th-century art and architecture, one common feature (born, perhaps, of the increasing 'indi-vidualisation' of the artist) is an accelerating profligacy of styles, which some are adept at turning on and off like a tap. Thus the crux of the problem in discussing Classicism in the 19th and 20th centuries is to decide whether or not the political, educational and academic structures which sustained such an approach to art and architecture are indeed essential for its survival. Were they were replaced by *different* structures, such as museums and galleries, to add to the perennial collecting instinct,[105] and the art-critical apparatus; or were such structures in fact fortuitous, and not of the *essence* of Classicism?

Indeed, the very *terminology* of 19th-century art leads to great confusion, although exactly the same can also be said for Baroque, Rococo and neo-classical.[106] Delacroix we can agree was a 'Romantic', but one much interested in Renaissance and Baroque traditions and in the heritage of the antique. Hence we find Walter Pach with a chapter called *The Classicism of Delacroix*,[107] which the author treats as *carte blanche* to play to the old game of 'spot the antique influence': we therefore find references to Pompeian wall painting, to Greek coins, and (more plausibly) to Homer; later, he does the same thing with Matisse, Duchamp-Villon and Barye. However, he manages to confuse the two ways of approaching the problem, namely 'spot the influence' and 'pendulum', as in his comment upon Matisse's remark that 'The further I go, the more I am convinced that there is a right and wrong in conduct and likewise in art': 'Matisse had witnessed the conflict of ideas among the various art movements of his time, and had come to the conclusion that they were not questions of personal taste but that they rested on fundamental, permanent truths.'[108] Are these the 'truths' of Classicism as style, or of Classicism as tradition?

Certainly, the 19th century offers great variety in terms of opportunities for *access* to the classical past, through publications, travel and academic structures. Mythological painting keeps going strongly, and there is a distinct revival of paintings on antique themes.[109] Similarly monumentality, often with a classical aspect (but sometimes a gothic one) is a constant theme in the arts in the 19th century; in landscape painting, for example, updated versions of the 17th-century vogue of Claude and Poussin, for 'classical landscape with figures', are very popular.[110]

The trouble is that the concept of *classic* gets mixed up with that of *romantic*, so that the term *romantic Classicism* is frequently used to denote a romantic *attitude* to classical or pseudo-classical *themes*. This is a Europe-wide phenomenon, seen not only in England and France, but in Germany and further north,[111] as well as in Italy, where Piranesi provides the best example of a romantic treatment of classical forms.[112]

A prime illustration of the nature of romantic Classicism is provided by the influence of the rediscovery of Greece[113] which, together with the Greek War of Independence, apparently separates classical *styles* from their traditional place as the end-product of *reason* – not emotion. Greek themes can henceforth be avowedly romantic in sentiment; and her people (whom Westerners had first come to know during the Greek Wars) not necessarily the only antique 'race of heroes'– witness Delacroix' transferal of this role to the arabs of North Africa. Again, the newly recognised problems facing the conscience of 19th-century Europe made the heroes and heroics of the past much less convincing or sustainable: the monuments erected to the heroes of the Napoleonic Wars are perhaps the last in Western Europe to adopt the ideal; and a growing realisation of the horrors of modern war[114] had the dual effect of moving artists away from idealism to realism or to a sanitised, 'romantic' treatment of the theme. The preparation for this derived from the increased sentimentalism of the previous century, and especially from the greater latitude with which some ancient authors were viewed. Homer, for example, the example of whose characters in no way fitted in with usual conceptions of civilised behaviour, began to be admired only in the 18th century, when the fierce passions and bloodthirsty deeds of the *Iliad* were found exciting rather than reprehensible.[115] Indeed, a Northern equivalent was discovered, or rather faked (by a Scot called MacPherson), to match him: namely *Ossian*.[116] The works of both partake more of romanticism than of Classicism.

## Academies and Change

In parallel to this shift in the nature of 'classic ground', academies also change their stance. They had begun in Renaissance Italy, as we have seen, as institutions for enshrining the 'rules' of good art, so that young artists and architects might receive training. Unfortunately, they gradually became rigid in their teaching and, in the perception of many artists, outdated in their views, exercising a tyranny which was strong because academies represented the 'official' view of art. An artist who followed academic ideas gained commissions, whereas one who flouted them remained in the wilderness.[117] Increasingly, as the 19th century advanced, European art fell into two camps antithetical to one another, with what was perceived as 'progressive' art being outside the academic fold. This is the case in Britain,[118] France,[119] and Italy.[120]

We can perhaps view the onset of 'modern' art, however defined, as in part a reaction to the 'academic institution and the formalist painting which was its expression' and a 'first

PIRANESI, ETCHING OF PAESTUM, 1760s

step in an analysis of the symbolic revolution caused by Manet and the Impressionists after him: the overthrowing of the social structures of the academic apparatus (ateliers, the Salons, etc) as well as its associated mental structures,'[121] – although Manet's art is replete with classical forms and ideas, if not a classical style. Similarly, Woelfflin's famous statement in favour of Classicism – namely his *Classic* Art – has itself been viewed as a reaction to the *non*-classical expression of artists like Courbet[122] – just as the very opposition to academic art was itself often seen as a political, not just an artistic, act.[123]

In the course of the late 18th century, then, and given the factors mentioned above together with the impact of truly Revolutionary art, Classicism degraded from a tradition to simply one of several possible styles, the tradition faltering badly because of a lack of confidence in its efficacy.[124] This was compounded by the democratisation of art, which involved both the removal of high art from its pedestal, and a growing uncertainty about what was or was not good taste – a weapon long wielded by the leisured, city-dwelling upper classes against the rest:

Requiring long cultivation, the absence of good taste betrays the parvenu, and requiring wealth and leisure it exposes the economically declassed. It is accessible only to those of a certain standard of living and upbringing, hardly to the poor and the provincial. Hence good taste becomes a canon of exclusiveness and lapses from it, whether of individuals or nations, are identified with social or cultural inferiority.[125]

Does the 20th-century academy still provide a useful training? Renoir's opinion, for example, was that 'C'est au musée qu'on apprend à peindre' – a conservative view that supports academies, since copying was a prime factor in the survival of classical form.

However, some artists believe that the academy is dead: Picasso, for example, has written:

. . . academic training in beauty is a sham. We have been deceived, but so well deceived that we can scarcely get back even a shadow of the truth. The beauties of the Parthenon, Venuses, Nymphs, Narcissuses are so many lies. Art is not the application of a canon of beauty but what the instinct and the brain can conceive beyond any canon. When we love a woman we don't start measuring her limbs . . . why cling desperately to everything that has already fulfilled its promise?

. . . To repeat is to run counter to spiritual laws; essentially escapism.[126]

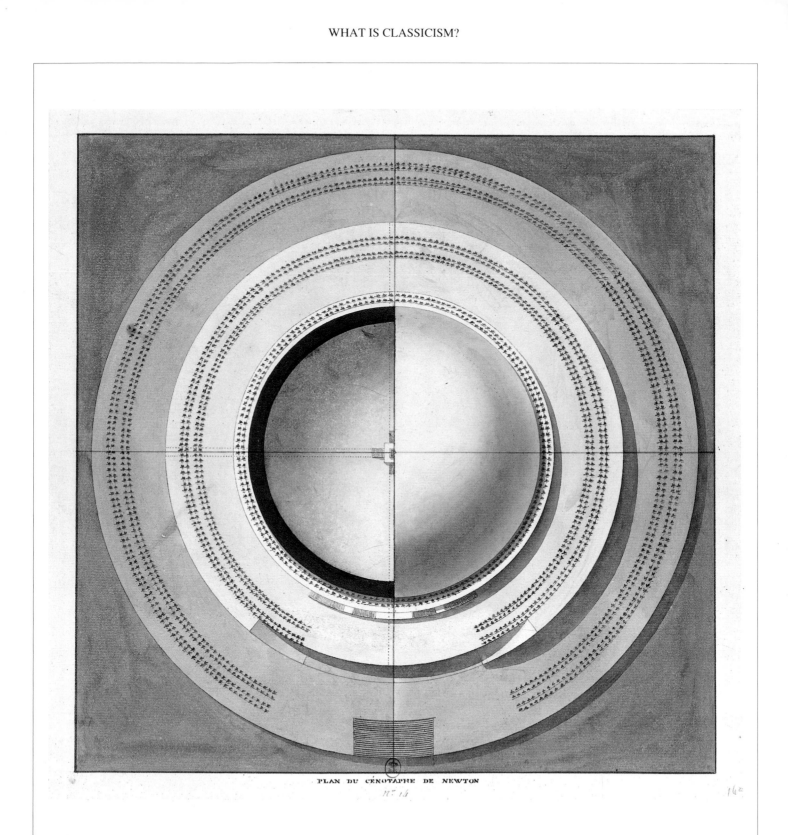

BOULÉE, PLAN OF CENOTAPH FOR NEWTON, INK AND WASH, 39 X 39 CM

Basic to Picasso's viewpoint is the overturning of established values, and the belief that a changing art has no eternal values. Novelty is of the essence. Marinetti makes essentially the same point, underlining that change undermines conventions, rather than enshrining them as Classicism had done: 'All is conventional in art. Nothing is absolute in painting. What was truth for the painters of yesterday is but a falsehood today' wrote Marinetti,[127] and it is clear that the break comes with Realism, if not with the full stop given to secular idealism by David and Ingres:

> To estimate the significance of Cubism one must go back to Gustave Courbet. This master, after David and Ingres had magnificently terminated a secular idealism, did not follow the example of the Delaroches and the Deverias, did not waste himself in servile repetition; he inaugurated a realistic impulse which runs through all modern efforts.[128]

Further, Boccioni, in his *Technical Manifesto of Futurist Sculpture,* of 1912, wrote that:

> The sculpture of every country is dominated by the blind and foolish imitation of formulas inherited from the past, an imitation encouraged by the double cowardice of tradition and facility Sculptors must convince themselves of this absolute truth: to continue to construct and want to create with Egyptian, Greek or Michelangelesque elements, is like wanting to draw water from a dry well with a bottomless bucket.[129]

And Boccioni's assessment of Rodin seems cruelly accurate:

> He bears in his sculpture a restless inspiration and a sweeping lyrical drive, which would be truly modern if Michelangelo and Donatello had not already possessed these qualities in almost identical form four hundred years or so before, and if they were used to animate a completely re-created reality.[130]

Other sculptors like Barye and Flaxman also sought inspiration, this time from the Greeks, with variable success;[131] but the majority wanted alternatives to classical beauty – self-expression and creation rather than the imitation of art and nature.[132]

This isolation of the classical as deceitful and out-dated, and hence irrelevant to the work of all right-thinking artists, tended not only to turn museums into mausolea where dead art was enshrined, but also to leave academies high and dry, without a viable *raison d'être*. After all, one of the strengths of Classicism had been its formulation into a teachable tradition; if people no longer wished to learn it, then survival was in doubt. In fact, Classicism is not dead, as the discussion of Post-Modernism will demonstrate

## Neo-Classicism in 19th-Century Architecture

During the 18th century, the knowledge of ancient architecture widened and deepened. The Italian Renaissance had known well only those works in Italy, Provence and Dalmatia; and although 17th-century travellers had brought back accounts of Egypt and Greece, these were replaced by the detailed and academic studies by Stuart & Revett of *The Antiquities of Athens* (2 vols, 1762 & 1787; French translation 3 vols, 1808–15), as well as by their *The Unedited Antiquities of Attica* of 1817.[133]

By 1800, a host of well-illustrated books, usually with measured drawings, was available on the Hellenistic ruins of Baalbek and Palmyra in the Middle East and on the Greek and Roman remains of Asia Minor, as well as on the early Greek temples at Paestum[134] and in Sicily. Architects therefore had at their disposition not only the extravagant antique Baroque of Baalbek, but also the stripped and stumpy austerity of the Greek Doric, and these considerably affected the focus of their theories.[135]

As available sources widened,[136] so attitudes changed. In the architectural version of the artistic and literary *querelle des anciens et des modernes*, the achievements of the ancients were usually accepted as a standard of excellence, and whether *modern* architecture was able to equal or to better them was a contentious point. Until the 17th century, the answer was generally no; for the 18th century, however, the achievements of modern civilisation led often to the answer yes, as in Britain.[137] The bewildering variety of antique architecture now revealed through books and prints helped provoke a new attitude to the architecture of the past, for the 'Renaissance tradition' with its interest in antique Classicism and its own development of new Classicisms, was now seen as but one of several possible styles worthy of imitation or adaptation. The range available was not only broader in style, but also in date; and it was probably the new interest in history which highlighted early and 'primitive' architecture – the equivalent of Flaxman's outline drawings, and of the vogue for Homer. The temples of Paestum, for example, well publicised through Piranesi's prints, showed awesomely heavy and solid members, and a simplicity of form which made some Roman architecture (and the 'baroque' excesses of some of Palladio's work) seem over-decorated and frivolous. In terms of emotional impact Piranesi's depictions are equivalent to the

C-N LEDOUX, SALT WORKS, ARC-ET-SENANS, FRANCE, 1775-79

grandeur of Egyptian architecture (as seen for example in Tesi's print of an Egyptian Hall, of 1787): only the style is different.[138]

As attitudes changed, so the relationship of architecture to its sources – the very nature of Classicism – also altered. Neoclassical architects, as averse to decoration as Jacques-Louis David was in his paintings, developed styles which, though recognisably inspired by the antique and especially by primitivism, were aggressively austere in their espousal of the basic geometrical shapes of cone, pyramid, cube and cylinder (with domes and tunnel vaults), of bare surfaces drenched in blinding light or inpenetrable shadow, and of immense scale. Named for its atmospheric megalomania *romantic* or *revolutionary Classicism,* it was small wonder that much of the most exciting material, such as that of Boullée and Ledoux, remained as drawings, for it could never have been built as it looked on paper.[139] Both men tried to develop a *speaking architecture,* by using motifs which proclaimed their purpose – such as pyramids for cemeteries, fasces for courts of justice. This was a brilliant idea, but too specific for the stylistic profligacy of the 19th century. Indeed, revolutionary Classicism is almost exclusively a French phenomenon, perhaps because of a French concern with basic principles in all the

arts, and certainly because of the closeness of art and politics during the Revolution, whereas the approach of other nationalities was usually more pragmatic and down-to-earth.

One opportunity for exercising such overheated imaginations was provided by the French competition for the bursary to study at the French Academy in Rome – the Grand Prix d'Architecture which, from the middle of the 18th century, encouraged a megalomania thought suitable to the grandeur of the ancient forms that were imitated. A good example of the genre is M J Peyre's design for a cathedral which, dating from 1753, displays strict symmetry, varied sources and an enormous scale. C-N Ledoux, a fashionable architect who attracted many rich commissions, developed this manner in his Paris toll-booths; because these were to collect royal taxes, 1785-9 was not an auspicious time to build them, and so it is not surprising that few survive. Luckily, however, his manner can be seen at his Royal Salt-Works at Arc-et-Senans (1775-9). The essentials of his manner can be seen in his houses for the Marquis de Saiseval, of 1786, and since destroyed: geometry is their foundation, with the use of the cube and the cylinder. The house at either end has in its pediment the Palladian motif (also known as the *serliana*), echoed on the *piano nobile,* while the windows in all three

J GANDY, *PUBLIC AND PRIVATE BUILDINGS . EXECUTED BY SIR J. SOANE BETWEEN 1780 AND 1815*, 1818

houses are simply cut onto the plain walls – no pediments or profiles, and no decoration. The *motifs* are recognisably antique-inspired, and the effect, while classical, is totally new, for Ledoux has no interest in being 'correct', only in being impressive. His work provides a pointer to one direction in which 19th-century Classicism might have developed, but did not. Such originality, analagous to that of Sir John Soane in England,[140] was meat too strong for the tame revivalists, who stuck to well-tried classical porticoes. The debate here was between the rationalism of structure and the superfluity of decoration; and it is characteristic of the 18th century that inspiration was found by theorists and architects such as Laugier and Soufflot not only in classical architecture, but in the Gothic as well.[141]

In England, architectural traditions were even broader, from the academic Classicism of Sir William Chambers and the brilliant and often highly decorated work of Robert Adam,[142] both of whom owed much to their study of the antique in Rome, to the much more original work of Sir John Soane, the oddity of some of whose designs reminds us that the Gothic was of growing importance in his day (1753-1837), whereas in France it was little used. In Britain, that is, the varieties of Classicism had to compete against not only the

Gothic, but also against the other styles imported by Empire, trade and travel – Egyptian, Chinese and Indian. Although chinoiserie was perhaps the first of the imported styles to be pan-European, being much used by Rococo artists, the others found little hold on the Continent. There are, nevertheless, pervasive examples of Classicism in 19th-century British architecture.[143]

Revolutionary Classicism exercised in France a liberating influence on architecture, as it did on painting and sculpture. The academic training of the Ecole des Beaux-Arts, fulfilled by competitions and prizes, kept the classicising torch burning from 1819 until 1968: some designs (such as Charles Garnier's Paris Opera, completed in 1875) adopt the drenched decoration of the pseudo-Baroque (sometimes called the 'Beaux-Arts' style, after the School), but many continue the stripped Classicism and gigantism of Ledoux, fuelled not only by theories of a neo-Greek manner, but also by a rebellion against the overt imitation of the antique. Julien Gaudet, professor at the Ecole des Beaux-Arts from 1894 to 1908, wrote of the strength of that school's reaction *against* what he saw as the classical ideal:

For a century, and throughout the world, the arts, and above all architecture, have been enfeebled by their subordination to archaeology; . . . in almost every other country, architecture is nothing more than an archaeological expression, a servile adaptation of illogical anachronisms . . . In Munich, they conjure up utilitarian Parthenons . . .[144]

This was a reference to the work of Leo von Klenze, a pupil of the French, whose Glyptothek (1816-34) and Propylaea (1846ff) proclaimed the Grecian style as fitting for Munich's museum complex. It was adopted for other German cities as well, conspicuously Berlin.[145] Yet Klenze was no stylistic bigot, for his Koenigsbau of 1826 for the Munich Residenz is in the Renaissance style, closely modelled on Palazzo Pitti in Florence. If German architecture provides one example of the continuing prestige of classical culture, then Russia offers another which, at least until after the Revolution, was imitative rather than original.[146]

But in spite of excursions into Greek and 'primitive' styles, and into 'stripped' Classicism and *architecture parlante*, Rome and the Renaissance tradition continued to provide the greatest quantity of solutions. There are no 18th-century examples of Greek-derived town planning in Europe, but plenty from the 'old' classical tradition: the Palladianism of Bath, the Place de la Carrière and Place Stanislas in Nancy, of 1750-7, and the Place de la Concorde in Paris (1753-70).

Gaudet's references to the noxious influence of archaeology might seem strange from a Professor teaching the classical tradition, but they underline the very different approach of many 19th-century architects to their material from that of their predecessors. For Alberti, Michelangelo, Ledoux and the rest, Antiquity was a storehouse of ideas and motifs, but 'correctness' was little prized, because they were in the business of producing *new* architecture. In a sense, they were helped in this because they could not see ancient buildings in their original glory: most had lost all their decoration and much of their claddings – so what they observed was itself a kind of 'stripped Classicism'! Indeed, Palladio was probably the only pre-19th-century student of the past who was interested in correctness, and this was because of his archaeological bent, rather than for direct translation into his own buildings. For the 19th century, however, the exact study of the past proved a burden: they learned about how ancient buildings had actually *looked,* and resurrected them in all their colour and sumptuous decoration – so that, ironically, exact knowledge of the past proved a barrier between them and their free-wheeling forbears, rather than adding crowning glory to a continuing tradition.

## Classicism and the Battle of the Styles

Just as Renaissance architects like Alberti and Palladio became famous for fitting antique ideas to works which could solve modern problems, so the 19th century, faced with an outburst of new *types* of building, did the same. As Pevsner has noted,[147] 19th-century architecture is evocative architecture – and hence the desire for churches to evoke the religious aura of the Middle Ages (Gothic), schools the attainments of the age of Pericles (Greek), or banks and offices the financial solidity of the Renaissance palazzo. However, such was 19th-century taste that there is no one style to fit one building type: a bank might be Greek, Gothic or Elizabethan, just like a teaching institution. Such historicism – that is, using an 'old' style to evoke a certain set of ideas or feelings – is itself a very old trick, which we shall see again in the work of the post-moderns. It is, therefore, in the public architecture – the big buildings – of the last 150 years that one sees Classicism and other styles at their best or worst. The same approach to the classical past survives into the 20th century, whether it be the great palazzo built by R Frank Atkinson for Selfridge's of London in 1908ff, the great Roman baths provided by McKim, Mead & White for Pennsylvania Station, New York in 1906-10 (demolished 1964), or J R Pope's Jefferson Memorial in Washington, commissioned in 1934.

The reasons for such variety are an increasing interest in history and a broadening of stylistic knowledge backed up by an increased rate of illustrated publications. We have seen that the late 18th- and 19th- century expansion of travel showed the West just how various were antique styles. It introduced them to other styles as well – Indian, Moorish and Chinese, for example – to add to the new interest in Romanesque and Gothic; so that there was indeed generated, as Mordaunt Crook puts it, a dilemma of style which continues to this day,[148] and which was clearly recognised at the time.[149]

With the growing interest in history, the broadened interest in the world, and the diminishing ability (and desire) of academies to set stylistic guidelines, the classical manners current since the Renaissance were seen as but one of a number of possible alternatives from which eclectically inclined architects might legitimately choose. Neo-Classicism (whether or not with a romantic admixture) did indeed liberate the 18th-century architect by demonstrating how broadly the notion of Classicism could be stretched,[150] but this did not of course solve the problem of which style (and which particular flavour) to choose - the Roman, Renaissance, Baroque, Romanesque, Greek or Gothic? A walk around any predominantly 19th-century city will illustrate the problem, which Peter Collins groups under the more general heading of *revivalism*.[151]

Just as Palladio's books are an important vehicle for the dissemination of his ideas, so the 18th- and 19th-century passion for studying material in a historical context generated books which confirmed the new and broader perspective. Although, as we have seen, this tended to dilute the impact of Classicism, the less exclusive attitude to the past which it entailed was especially valuable for throwing light on the hitherto generally ignored Middle Ages. Between 1811 and 1820, Seroux d'Agincourt produced the six folio volumes, containing 325 plates, of his *Histoire de l'art par les monuments, depuis sa décadence jusqu'à son renouvellement au XVI, pour servir de suite à l'histoire de l'art chez les anciens,* the title of which accurately reflects his intention of filling in the gaps in the history of art as then understood. For the first time students had available, through his plates, a good survey of the subject – the ancestor, perhaps, of Sir Banister Fletcher's modern architectural classic, *A History of Architecture*. Now, for the first time, the work of the Middle Ages was presented as worthy of attention, and as part of a development, rather than as an aberration from the True Path.

Although there are some conspicuous and important exceptions, this focus on the past was responsible for an almost complete lack of interest in what we might now call 'social architecture' – in designing buildings for ordinary people. Classicism was the vehicle for the grand public statement designed to impress and to survive, whereas workaday buildings, especially houses, were not. The academic tradition must also share some responsibility for this: it had nothing to offer, unless it was the facadism of speculative building – the doorcases and pediments, windows and finials stuck onto the simple box-like construction of Georgian terraces. Indeed, its strength appeared to confirm the supremacy of backward-looking Classicism – and this in spite of the Industrial Revolution, which had offered some competition for this received view with technical and engineering schools, just as Romanticism perhaps led to an interest in planning at the same time as it fostered other non-classical styles. The French *Grand Prix d'Architecture,* which guaranteed study in Rome, sustained the 'never-never' tradition also indulged in by the 'revolutionary architects' – ideal buildings, sometimes megalomaniac, and never intended for construction – which gradually became further removed from the realities of actual architecture and life. A recent critic has characterised all this

as 'authoritarian traditionalism, its emphasis on general and abstract theory rather than on conditions of specific and actual practice, its tendency to limit its subject-matter to monumental problems of a national and civic kind'[152] – and indeed, there remains to this day a strong strain of building 'castles in the air', to be seen in the heroics of the architectural competition, itself essentially a 19th-century invention. Not surprisingly, the *Grands Prix* tradition flourished under Fascism: a good example – which remained on the drawing board – is Albert Speer's Grosse Halle for Berlin, a gigantic complex the centrepiece of which would have been a domed hall of 220 metres internal height, the whole scheme looking like a cross between the Pantheon in Rome, Bramante's project for St Peter's and (for the colonnades) the Altare della Patria.[153]

Another new invention of the 19th century was to be an important vehicle for historicism. The large international exhibition was a particularly conspicuous type of public architecture where, alongside some pioneering work in industrial architecture (such as that of Paxton at the Great Exhibition of 1851, in London), Classicism was much in evidence, perhaps because of the atmosphere of august stability and millenial virtue it could add to what were often by their very nature temporary constructions. Here again, perhaps, we also see the equation good architecture = classicising architecture.[154] Such fairs were used as the vehicle for an economic, patriotic, and (sometimes) imperial message; and fittingly it was Classicism that was their usual style – 'to inspire a reverence toward the pure ideal of the ancients'[155] because this is exactly how the Greeks and Romans had used *their* architecture, whether in an alien environment, or in the very seat of their power. The Valle Giulia, outside the walls of Rome, was the site for a grand exhibiton, one of the few remains of which is now the British School at Rome, established in 1901: it is fitting that this institution, imitating the French tradition of the *Grands Prix* and housing scholars in art and architecture, should be in a neo-Palladian style. Louis Sullivan, commenting on such exhibitions in the USA, railed against what he called a 'virus, a selling campaign of the bogus antique,' and concluded that 'we now have the abounding freedom of Eclecticism, the winning smile of taste, but no architecture.'[156] Much of Sullivan's own work is an effective critique of Beaux-Arts copying precisely because he re-inteprets the classical past and produces therefrom forward-looking rather than retrogressive solutions.

Luckily, however, exhibitions were public platforms not only for visions of classical beauty, such as the Nashville version of the Parthenon (and that in full colour), but also for new building methods (the Crystal Palace, 1851) and new building types (the Eiffel Tower, 1889). In other words, Classicism had competition – the more so since the presentation of Classicism was usually in the Beaux-Arts manner, which stood up poorly against what were often strikingly innovative new designs, sometimes couched in new materials and employing new building techniques. Classicism was not to be totally inimical to new views of the nature and resources of architecture, as Mies van der Rohe would demonstrate; but the very introduction of new building methods raised the very question of whether classical styles were suitable for the modern age – a debate which continues today around the question of Post-Modernism

## Classicism in 20th-Century Painting and Sculpture

Although it is not difficult to trace in painting a continuing interest in the classical from the Cubists up to the present day, the strength of the tradition is in doubt, partly at least because the *range* of sources now used is very broad. There is no better illustration of this than the work of Henry Moore, 'the last sculptor of the Renaissance'[157] – the man whose 'most ambitious figure sculptures often appear to be modern, hyperborean interpretations of the Elgin Marbles, grandly rejuvenating the venerable British dialogue with classical art and fulfilling the requirement of numerous public commissions to provide something at once old and new'.[158] In his work, abstraction goes side by side with continual figure-drawing, and his images 'almost always has a specific model in the human body.[159] However, it is interesting that, after a scholarship in Italy in 1925, he came back confused, and only found a 'way out' when he discovered the Chacmool reclining figure from Chichen Itza (Museo Nacional de Antropologia, Mexico City). In 1935 he 'listed the great sculpture of the world as Sumerian, Early Greek, Etruscan, Ancient Mexican, Fourth and Twelfth Dynasty Egyptian, Romanesque and early Gothic'[160] – but *not* classical art in any form. Indeed, he did not visit Greece until he was 53 years of age, perhaps because of antipathy to what he thought Greece represented. As he wrote in 1961:

> There was a period when I tried to avoid looking at Greek sculpture of any kind. And Renaissance. When I thought that the Greek and the Renaissance were the enemy, and that one had to throw all that over and start again from the beginning of primitive art. It's only perhaps in the last ten or 15 years that I began to know

how wonderful the Elgin Marbles are.

The case of Cézanne underlines the same point. While it is surely correct to write in general terms that Cézanne's paintings 'are marked by a sensation of permanence in a world of silence and classical tranquility',[161] Theodore Reff has demonstrated[162] that Cézanne's famous remark about wanting 'to do Poussin again after nature' is in fact a distortion by his classicising commentators. He did indeed venerate Poussin – but no more than Veronese, Rubens or Delacroix. A much better assessment of his relationship with the past is his comment in a letter to Roger Marx in 1905 that 'To my way of thinking, one doesn't substitute oneself in the place of the past, but only add a new link in the chain.' Picasso might have said as much; certainly, he also has 'classic' periods, but these are 'a revision of antiquity in terms of modern experience: he saw beyond the technical excitement of solving a pictorial equation in terms of second-rate Roman sculpture to the point where he found in the pleasures of domesticity a monumental and universal artform.'[163] Certainly, Picasso's oeuvre is very diverse: he can turn styles on and off like a tap, but appears to have no consistent interest in classical *values* as opposed to classical forms and motifs. To demonstrate this, one needs only to compare *Les Demoiselles d'Avignon* with *Guernica,* the *Vollard Suite* and the *Las Meninas* series: all are based on grand themes from European art, but the continuing importance of Classicism for him is in doubt, and a more thoroughgoing re-use of the past is to be seen in the work of Giorgio de Chirico. Nevertheless, De Chirico distorts classical values in his constant search for metaphysical enigmas. One of his most famous works, *The joys and enigmas of a strange hour* (1913, Santa Barbara, California) is built up like a Poussin, with classicising architecture and spatial structure, and a quotation of colossal size from the *Sleeping Aphrodite* in the Vatican Belvedere. But the point of this painting (De Chirico refers to his interest in *plastic loneliness*) is far from the idealised, life-enhancing normality of the 17th century. Stylistically, De Chirico's settings may look like the works of classically-oriented Italian architects between the Wars: but he seeks another reality, one of psychological tension and alienation, rather than that sublimation of everyday reality which true Classicism provides.

Idealism and its associated values, and not classical forms, are therefore what must be addressed in any study of modern Classicism. Quotations and adaptations from the past, whether of antique sculpture or of Poussin or Ingres, are frequent in 20th-century art and architecture, but idealism is generally

GIORGIO DE CHIRICO, *ITALIAN SQUARE*, 1921, OIL ON CANVAS, 55 X 75 CM

lacking, because of the insistent desire to represent the here and now. One critic squares this particular circle by using terms such as 'ideal realism' or writing of artists who 'capture the spirit of Classicism while disregarding its letter',[164] – which emphasises the extent to which the parameters of Classicism and the classical tradition have to be moved if we are to encompass within a broader 'Classicism' artists such as RB Kitaj, Lincoln Perry or Eric Fischl as well as the more direct revivalists such as Giorgio de Chirico, Edward Schmidt or Thomas Cornell.

The break with true idealism comes in the 19th century.[165] Already, with Ingres, it is difficult to view his production as totally classical, for there are frequently admixtures of Romanticism and even semi-realism. Puvis de Chavannes keeps alive the Italian tradition of monumental fresco painting, but tends toward two-dimensionality; Degas begins in the Ingres manner, but quickly develops in other directions; both Millet and Renoir are much inspired by the classical tradition throughout their working life, but they are not constrained by it. In sculpture, a similar break occurred, epitomised by the difficulties Rodin had with 'traditional' monumental forms, and by the startlingly new solution he eventually arrived at with his *Balzac*.[166]

Art education, following changes in society and the artist's relationship to it, is one reason for this radically different attitude to the past. The decline in prestige of the academy is another. So that while architects still draw and admire ancient buildings and site layouts, it is no longer the practice in many art schools to draw from the antique, or indeed to work at all in what we may call the Renaissance tradition of ideal, figurative art. Post-Modernism may be changing this – but not much. The preoccupations of our century are different, and any attempt to encourage Classicism (as did the Comte de Caylus, an influential theorist and amateur in 18th-century France) by setting antique, ennobling subjects for artists to interpret would be met with incomprehension and derision. Our educational horizons have also changed, and by any measure the intensive study of the classics has declined, in spite of the greater numbers now travelling to classical lands. I shall suggest of Mussolini that his brand of Classicism was so powerful because styles were yoked to ideas. But where are our classical ideas/ideals today? Where is that set of agreed values hitherto required for the commissioning and acclamation of classicising art and architecture? From this perspective the traditions of Renaissance art, that sturdy support of Classicism, are dormant or dead, the result of a deliberate act by Modernism. The post-modernists would have us believe in their resurrection, but the very fragmentation of contemporary art makes long-term trends difficult to discern – or to accept even when shouted from the roof-tops by supporters with axes to grind and money to be made.

Perhaps the crux of the distinction between 'traditional' Classicism and its modern-day variants in whatever medium is the altered importance of Greece and Rome, and the distinction already made several times in this book between Classicism as ideal and Classicism as style and motif, with the former infinitely more important than the latter. Essential for earlier periods, does modern Classicism still require their apparatus (the orders for architecture; mythology and idealism for art), or can it survive on style and motif alone? Frequently not, if we forget for the moment the post-modernists: the Purists and Futurists of the 1920s, for example, sought their own kind of *tabula rasa*.

Equally seriously, and remembering that accumulation is characteristic of the classical tradition, does modern Classicism look forward, or only backward? If forward, then surely Cézanne and Mies van der Rohe are valid role models for its continuance. Or, differently phrased, is contemporary Classicism action and hence 'progress', or simply a deadening reaction to the progressive and exciting art and architecture of our century? The answer depends on one's perspective. Galerie Gmurzynska in Cologne, for example, could put on a large show in 1981 entitled *Klassische Moderne*, and include artists such as Delaunay, Arp, Kandinsky, Léger and Schwitters, without so much as a hint at a definition: are these just 'good' artists, or are they truly classical in any meaningful sense?

This unwillingness to commit themselves to meaning – whilst the search for it is undoubtedly one of their aims – is the ironic crux of the failure of many moderns and post-moderns boldly to interpret and re-use elements of the classical tradition, and the reason why their 'Classicism' is of the weaker, style/motif variety: that is, it sometimes lacks ideas. As Pommer comments, the use of history in painting and sculpture:

> . . . is a source of infinite possibilities, along with nature, science, dreams, etc. In architecture it has either been taken as a storehouse of forms useful for the next battle but without deeper meanings . . . or it has been seen as the repository of an ominously undefinable 'tradition' . . . to be interpreted only by those who know either their Classicism or their Marx and so can use history against all attempts to escape its laws.[167]

## Modern Architecture and Classicism

'A building by Mies van der Rohe', writes Jameson, 'may look modern enough, but underneath the flashy exterior is the same old classical temple, sometimes standing up and sometimes lying down, but always keeping to the same classical symmetries, the same classical concern with simple rhythmic repetitions.[168] This description introduces the crux of our problem with the term *classical* in this century – namely, what are the basic characteristics which a work must possess before it can be so termed? Must it look like an ancient building, with columns, pediments and the rest? Or are the general classical ideals of balance and restraint sufficient? Just how 'historical' must it be to qualify for the epithet *classical?* The question is particularly relevant today as, depending on which side of the fence you reside, the works of Mies represent on the one hand the acme of purity for the modern movement and, on the other, the best example of all that was wrong with Modernism – namely pure in form, but without relation to either site or function; that is, buildings unfitted to the world they inhabit. This is the position adopted by passionate post-modernists, for whom Robert Venturi's witticism *Less is a bore* (coined in 1961), and taken from Mies' own *Less is more,* sets the tone. However, Venturi does not like to be labelled a post-modernist, and subsequently retracted the remark.

Fortunately for the richness of the medium, historicism did not enter the 20th century as the only possible recourse for architecture,[169] Geoffrey Scott's *Architecture of Humanism,* for example, first published in 1914, has as its aim 'to formulate the chief principles of classical design in architecture'. Scott demolishes various fallacies – the romantic, the picturesque, the naturalistic, and so on – which he believes detract from the business of good architecture. His concern, therefore, with the 'baggage' of Classicism (so bound up in the 19th-century fallacies he details) is slight; instead, he suggests that 'By the direct agency of Mass and Space, Line and Coherence upon our physical consciousness, architecture communicates its value as an art', and concludes that, with impedimenta removed, the study of the classical and classicising past can be the better studied. This strange book might contain much special pleading, but it is refreshing to find a theorist with so little use for theories. Indeed, he suggests in the epilogue to the 1924 edition that they 'made the chatter on the scaffolding of the Tower of Babel'. For the future, Scott's book signals a turning in the classical tradition toward a stripped Classicism unshackled by the Beaux-Arts tradition – toward, that is, an architecture of classicising innovation. This is exemplified in the early ideas of Le Corbusier, who stated that modern architecture is the result of a veritable revolution:

> Construction has undergone innovations so great that the old 'styles' which still obsess us, can no longer clothe it; the materials employed evade the attentions of the decorative artist. There is so much novelty in the forms and rhythms furnished by these constructional methods . . . that we can no longer close our minds to the true and profound laws of architecture.[170]

It must be emphasised that this is not a plea against the fundamentals of Classicism (witness Le Corbusier's reverence for the classical past), but rather against its later mis-use.

The best modern examples of the innovations resulting from this 'stripped Classicism' point of view are Le Corbusier's Pavillon de l'Esprit Nouveau and Mies van der Rohe's Barcelona Pavilion, the former at the Paris Exhibition of 1925, the latter at the Barcelona Exhibition of 1929. Such buildings, clearly of great quality and influence, call into question the very complexion of 20th-century Classicism.[171] Although very different, Mies' and Le Corbusier's demonstration pieces have all the hallmarks of Classicism in the abstract, such as simplicity, restraint, understatement, cubic integrity and basic rhythms. In Mark Wigley's words,[172] like the classicists, the modernists 'articulated the surface of a form in a way that marked its purity. They restored the very tradition they attempted to escape, replacing the classical skin with a modern skin but not transforming the fundamental condition of the architectural object. Architecture remained an agent of stability.' But unfortunately, from the point of view of public acceptance, their works sometimes lacked those familiar and friendly literal symbols of the tradition – recognisable columns, capitals, pediments or detailing – which had been the mainstay of the tradition for everyone except the great innovators such as Ledoux or Soane, and which make Ledoux-like buildings such as the Lincoln memorial in Washington (of 1914-20) so popular. The tradition of Mies can still be strong in contemporary architecture, as in his National Gallery in Berlin, of 1968. This is a veritable temple of art, of which Schinkel himself might have been proud (as Mies himself believed); but it has been criticised for its sophisticated abstraction: a beautiful abstract space it might be, but it does not *signify* museum or gallery, any more than it seems designed expressly to contain works of art.[173]

Against this view one might quote the case of the Greek temple which, since ancient times, has been a paradigm for the museum; for this reason, perhaps, Skidmore, Owings & Merrill's very Miesian addition to the Allbright-Knox Art Gallery at Buffalo, of 1962[174] sits confidently on its podium next to the veritable temples of the original neo-classical structure of 1905. Is not a building by Mies van der Rohe, as Jameson writes, 'the same old classical temple'? Certainly, America took to the Miesian style because, in Scully's words,[175] 'it was simplified, pure, clean, generalised, reasonable, abstract: the colonial house all over again'.

A constant problem with classical art and architecture is that, although its fundamentals are basically rational and hence teachable, it spawns as much bad work as any other value system. And it must be said that Mies has not been well served by his 'followers', 'who saw minimalism not as a medium for elegant simplification and technical perfection, but only as an opportunity for cheaper, easier, and therefore more profitable real-estate development.'[176] Mies himself was well aware of this; as he remarked at the end of his life, 'We showed them what to do. What the hell went wrong?' The answer is a simple one – namely that not all architecture can be good architecture, especially if built to a formula rather than as the result of inspiration; and, as we have seen, the formulaic propensities of Classicism (in whatever medium) lend themselves dangerously easily to 'painting by numbers'. Thus the utopian dream of a pure modern Classicism became – at least for its critics – a nightmare of generic boxes.

For most observers, the work of Mies does indeed fit within a classical canon,[177] for the reasons Jameson gives. And it is not difficult to trace the sources of such Classicism, even if we begin only with Louis Sullivan's Guaranty Building in Buffalo, New York (1894-5), which looks like a tall version of a Renaissance palazzo, as an interesting intermediary between the French Beaux-Arts tradition and the Bauhaus. Indeed, a good case can be made for the skyscraper, far from being a radical departure from the European tradition, as being intimately linked to it.[178]

But 20th-century Classicism is not restricted to Miesian minimalism, for not everyone was happy to accept it as simply a style to be used because it was aesthetically pleasing; for some, Classicism was to carry a message – to be evocative, to be speaking architecture. The revolutionary movements of the 20th century – Fascism in Italy and Germany, and Communism in Russia – adopted varieties of Classicism for political reasons, and have thereby gone counter to the mainstream of current artistic ideals, not least in their historicising and deliberate nationalism.[179] As Osbert Lancaster tells us, there is little difference between the proletarian and the fascist, because they 'both labour under the same misapprehension - that political rhetoric is a sufficient substitute for genuine architectural inspiration'.[180] If so, this is because the use to which they put architecture was similar – witness Hitler's desire to evoke, through the solidity and historical references in his architecture and town planning, the longevity of the Reich itself.[181] As Hitler's words reproduced in bronze on the facade of the Munich Haus des Deutschen Kunst have it, *KEIN VOLK LEBT LAENGER ALS DIE DOKUMENTE SEINER KULTUR. 11 SEPT 1935. ADOLF HITLER*. If, indeed, 'No people lives longer than the documents of its culture', then this helps explain why so much of the art of the Third Reich is deliberately reminiscent of earlier European (especially German) art, as in the work of Adolf Wissel, Wilhelm Petersen or Karl Diebitsch.[182] Such products are not new in manner, but blatantly reactionary: they are *against* modern art, not a version of it[183] – a phenomenon which many would argue occurs in post-modern architecture.

In Italy, Classicism could be espoused as a truly national style, as the very continuation of the Roman Empire in Rome, so it is not surprising to find the classical manner much favoured – never more so than in the *Altare della Patria*, or *Vittoriano*, or *Typewriter*, begun in 1885 to celebrate Italian Reunification, which looms over the whole of the city of Rome like a giant incubus. During the dictatorship of Mussolini, Rome was used for public ceremonies as a setting redolent of political might, whereby the City's millenial monuments could suggest the inevitability of Fascism's survival. In 1925, he set out his programme: 'Within five years, Rome must appear marvellous to all the peoples of the world – vast, orderly, powerful, as in the time of the empire of Augustus . . . You [the Governor of Rome] shall continue to free the trunk of the great oak from everything that darkens it', This he did, destroying large swathes of mediaeval and later Rome for ever.[184] Mussolini's manipulation of Rome almost as a theatre set was no more than Augustus, Charlemagne or the Papacy before him had done. Indeed, the attitude of all these men to the classical past demonstrates that it is ideas as well as architecture that make Classicism powerful. Like a true emperor, therefore, Mussolini undertook vast building and planning projects such as the raising of the Roman galleys from Lake Nemi, and the construction of a monumental complex for a (cancelled) 1942 *Olimpiade della Civiltà* at EUR (*Esposizione Universale di Roma*).

Fascist architecture now seems more complicated – let alone of higher quality - than some are prepared to concede, its range of sources being much broader than Classicism alone.[185] Unfortunately, it has not received the scholarly and critical attention it deserves: that is to say, loathing for Fascism has entailed loathing for the architecture and art espoused by Fascism, and a potentially valuable link in the tradition of Classicism thereby remains untested. Leon Krier, writing on the 'unfashionable' Speer, suggests that this confusion between architecture and regime has even sullied Classicism itself: 'I can only explain the misjudgement [about Speer's quality as an architect] by the fact that Classical Architecture was implicitly condemned by the Nuremberg Tribunal to an even heavier sentence than Speer.'[186] For many post-modernists, any taint of fascism in architecture provokes a knee-jerk reaction. Jencks, for example, calls the Palazzo della Civiltà at EUR near Rome (built in 1942) 'deflowered Classicism and endlessly repeated blank forms.'[187] The problem here is not, I suggest, with the quality of the architecture, but with the illogicality of the argument: architecture varies from good to bad, but people transfixed by historicism (which will be dealt with at greater length below) are frequently misled by what might be called associationism. A moment's thought should convince us that the architecture of the 1930s in Germany and Italy can and must be considered on its considerable architectural merits (many of them classical ones); and further, that it is as illogical to dismiss the work of Speer (on the grounds that he worked for Hitler) as it is to dismiss Wagner because he was Hitler's favourite composer.

**Planning the Modern City**

The Fascists in Italy and Germany were especially conscious of the need for planning an environment in which their buildings could attain their full significance; and, for both, it was antiquity which provided the model. Certainly, the town planning dimension is a constant in the history of architectural theory, especially in times of growing population, when the old has to be adapted (or done away with) to make way for the new; but it is widely acknowledged that the population explosion of our century, together with a transport-led migration to suburbia, has created acute problems in the management of urban space. This is not the place for even a short survey of the history of town planning: suffice it to say that there is a clear dichotomy in 20th-century approaches to the question – a dichotomy that provides an introduction to the

MUSEO DELLA CIVILTÀ ROMANA, EUR, ROME, 1942

dispute between Modernism and Post-Modernism which will be discussed in detail below.

Auguste Perret, intoxicated early in the century by the coming of the machine age, proposed the 'City of Towers' with a radical separation of people and housing from vehicles and industry; the only way to improve the environment under this scheme, so enthusiastically preached by Le Corbusier, was to build tower blocks on a gigantic – and not just a monumental – scale of 60 storeys or more. This approach was associated with Modernism in architectural style, as seen by its acceptance in Hitchcock & Johnson's *The International Style,* the influential handbook to the movement first published in 1932.

Although such gigantism may well work in new-built cities, many regard it as distasteful because of its anonymity, lack of human scaling, and complete break with the past. The alternative is a return to the European tradition, begun in the Greek and Hellenistic world, and refined especially in the 17th and 18th centuries, which gives due prominence to public buildings not only by separating them from housing and placing them on grand axes, agoras or rond-points, but also by scaling down the housing into manageable units. The results can be seen in Leon Krier's admirable Royal Mint

Square Housing project of 1974, or in the much more ambitious La Villette competition in 1976, the classical dignity of which would not have seemed unusual either to Ledoux, himself the designer of an ideal city for La Chaux-de-Fonds, to Pierre Patte who wished to redesign Paris, or to the designers of Bath. Significantly, Krier's re-interpretation of tradition extends only to the planning, the elevations being modernist (*not* post-modernist) classical, and similar in type to, for example, Rob Krier's White House on the Ritterstrasse in Berlin (1977-80).

How relevant can classically derived town planning be to the problems of post-industrial societies? Should we be inspired by visions which have more to do with ideal cities, with bijou settings like Nancy, Bath, Covent Garden or a painting by Poussin, than with an untidy world teeming with dingy relics of an unplanned past and the glossy buildings of Modernism? Is Classicism in town planning a viable alternative to make-and-mend, or simply an historicist vision?

## Modernism and Post-Modernism in Architecture

*Post-Modernism* is a term which has already appeared in this account of the changing nature of Classicism. It is a useful jargon term, applied in literature,[188] philosophy and

ROB KRIER, RITTERSTRASSE, BERLIN-KREUZBERG, 1977-80

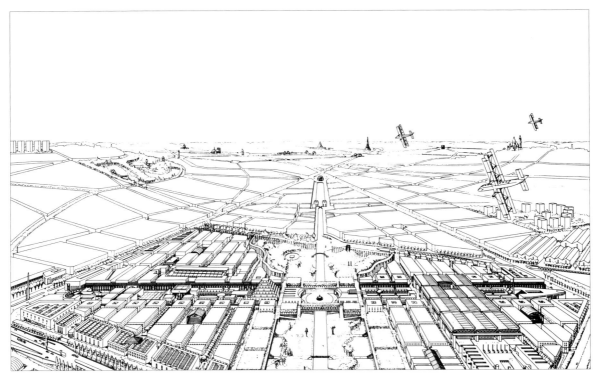

LEON KRIER, QUARTIER DE LAVILLETTE, 1976

aesthetics.[189] It can be, and indeed is, applied to painting and sculpture, but I shall concentrate on architecture, where it was first used as an antonym to Modernism in the early 1970s: for it is here that this latest 'ism' has raised the most interest.

Before going any further, however, it should be pointed out that Post-Modernism is not necessarily a movement, much less a style, although it is certainly (like Modernism) international, rather than restricted to one or two countries: the very structure of the word indicates that it comes after Modernism, but commentators say little about what this might imply (unlike, for example, Classicism, which carries with it a baggage of attitudes and presuppositions). In truth, there is plentiful evidence that Post-Modernism is a buzz-word, constantly abused to the point that it becomes near-meaningless. A good example of this is a recent book entitled *The Postmodern presidency: the office after Ronald Reagan*. There is certainly room for some sceptical PhD student to examine the propagation and flourishing of the notion of Post-Modernism as an important example of architectural politics. For to attempt a straightforward art-historical account of the phenomenon is probably to invite failure, so amorphous is the concept.

Significantly, in an age when the visual arts are so often treated with disdain by all but practitioners and professional critics, the very concept of Post-Modernism in architecture has aroused interest not only amongst the media, but also the general public. This is of course as it should be: everyone lives in an environment, whether urban or not, and is therefore a consumer of architecture; and concern for its quality has been a dominant theme of our century amongst sociologists and psychiatrists as well as artistic practitioners. The pot has been kept well on the boil not only by the architectural press, but also by the high profile now given to architectural competitions, especially those for contentious locations such as the National Gallery extension in London, the Portland Public Service Building in Oregon, or the new Parliament House for Canberra; while exhibitions, especially the Venice Biennale of 1980, give a wide currency to new ideas.

Post-modern buildings, briefly defined by Charles Jencks as 'buildings . . . rooted in place and history, unlike the buildings of their immediate predecessors',[190] have caught the attention of the public, and have provided the architectural profession with two main positions, widely separated, which they can adopt. On the one side is the tradition of the modern movement, an approach to architecture predicated upon the new materials and methods of industrial production but at the

43

QUINLAN TERRY, RICHMOND RIVERSIDE, 1983-88

same time (as we have seen) not necessarily anti-classical; on the other is Post-Modernism, which might equally accurately have been dubbed anti-Modernism,[191] since its essential characteristic in whatever medium is that it sees itself as a reaction *against* Modernism rather than a continuation of it, bolstered by the widespread belief that Modernism itself has failed: 're-vivalists view the modern movement as an unfortunate aberration in the tradition of Western architecture, one which precludes cultural continuity or social expression.[192] In this regard, it is characteristic that Charles Jencks should, after a brief introduction, begin one of his books on Post-Modernism[193] with a chapter entitled 'The death of modern architecture'. Or, broadening the argument to place architecture correctly within the context of urban planning, 'Le Corbusier, the Rasputin of this tale, . . . represents the counter-tradition [to benevolent anarchism] of authoritarian planning, the evil consequences of which are ever with us.'[194] Jencks, for example, castigated the work of Alison and Peter Smithson for 'anti-traditionalism'and a 'machine aesthetic'[195] in spite of their awareness of the need for a modern version of the humanising symbolism seen, for example, in 18th-century Bath.

The basis for this apparently negative approach lies in Post-Modernism's attitude to tradition in general and Classicism in particular; for if Modernism was indeed an embarrassing (and now dead?) interruption to the continuity of tradition, then Post-Modernism can be presented as no less than a continuation of the avant-garde[196] rather than (as it is in the eyes of some) a strange and pale attempt to resurrect classical ideals unsuited to modern life. For after the International Style, after Modernism, what were the choices available, beyond 'a stripped Classicism and the vernacular tradition?'[197] Are we perhaps being forced to choose between the elitist mode of the classical tradition, and the vernacular manner which, by definition, distorts it?

One answer provided by some post-modernist architecture is a revival of historicism – of a devoted adherence to the great facades, motifs and sometimes structures of the European heritage. We should not be surprised by this return to the past: after all, historicism as an approach (perhaps as a substitute for style?) haunts much of 19th-century art and architecture; while its adjuncts – engravings, photographs, slides, the press – have made the past much more accessible than it has ever been. The study of art and architectural history (and perhaps of history in all its forms) are spin-offs of historicism, and the 'presence of the past' – its importance for the future, as well as the title of the 1980 Venice Biennale – has long been recognised.

Another answer, related to the first, is the re-establishment of ornament as a worthy part of architecture, in deliberate reaction to Modernism's view that it is 'aesthetically retarded, morally reprehensible, or simply the affliction of people who don't know better.'[198] The historical context in which one can discuss the use and mis-use of ornament is fascinating, because it seems to many to impinge upon morality itself: structure is good, decoration (if not carefully controlled, and exactly appropriate) is bad. Past centuries have had few problems with generating ornament suitable to classicising buildings, but to the modern movement ornament of any kind was truly anathema, because it was equated with immorality. The most extreme statement of the case is by Adolf Loos who, in his *Ornament and Crime,* of 1908, opined that 'The evolution of culture is synonymous with the removal of ornament from utilitarian objects.' As a reaction, Peter Fuller believes 'the destruction of ornament within the modernist movement was one of the cultural crimes of our age.'[199] This is not the place to enlarge on this argument; but part of the outrage generated by some of the more blatant ornamentalism in post-modern architecture must be seen within a moral dimension, as well as within an architectural and historical one. Unfortunately, to take a moral stance is frequently to obscure the architectural issues – although some would argue that morality cannot be separated from the social art of architecture. Indeed, it has been suggested that *ornamentalism* is a better way of describing the nature of contemporary architecture than *Post-Modernism,* a far more ambiguous term.[200]

The crux of the continuing debate on Post-Modernism, however, is just how the past is to be used in constructing the future – especially, the modernists might add, because we are separated from that past by industrial methods of construction. Battle-lines have been drawn, and the debate – or more usually polemic – between the two sides can be acrimonious. For the modernists, Post-Modernism oscillates between facadism and facile pastiche, using the past as a crutch rather than an inspiration. For the post-modernists, the evidence of the failure of the modern movement is all around us – cities and buildings without meaning, lacking a human scale, and nurturing a host of social and political problems. Certainly, many people actually like post-modernist architecture, seeing it as familiar, traditional, and of human scale, in contrast with the impersonality, the startling novelty and the colossal scale of much of the architecture of our modern cities. Nev-

CHARLES MOORE, PIAZZA D'ITALIA, NEW ORLEANS, LOUISIANA, 1975-80

ertheless, the proposed cure does not fit the disease: Bruno Zevi suggests that 'Nobody . . . could believe that a city today, with all its problems, can be assembled by montage, or even more accurately, by a pastiche of elements from the past. Post-Modernism doesn't propose a modern city, a territorial asset. It proposes a series of drawings . . . a series of facades, like those in Venice.'[201]

A prominent illustration of the dilemma of just *how* to use the past is provided by the work of Quinlan Terry. We have seen how its values and motifs have been continually re-interpreted into a modern idiom, and how the orders of architecture have usually been modified to suit new stylistic or structural goals. But what if one simply ignores the 20th century, and proclaims the sacrosanctity of the orders? Pastiche is therefore the stance of Quinlan Terry, the architect of the recent neo-Georgian Howard Building at Downing College, Cambridge: 'Terry reverted to pre-neo-classical Classicism and his building evokes an early 18th-century country house by some amateur architect who has made the Grand Tour', writes Hugh Honour.[202] Such rigidity – similar to the standpoint of Viollet-le-Duc in the 19th century – equates with Neville Quarry's epithet for Post-Modernism of *post–mortemism*, when it attempts to take architecture way back beyond steel, concrete and glass to before the Industrial Revolution – historicism putting back the clock, so to speak. Again, the public acceptance of some post-modernist architecture presents a new version of an old dilemma, because that which is popular is not necessarily good, even in a popularist age. For example, it surely takes special pleading to see Terry's Richmond Riverside development as analogous to anything other than Disneyland: both are false precisely because they are unrelated to the social or ideological fabric of the Modern Age: they quote, but they do not believe, so that the result resembles a picture postcard, mis-located in a modern setting. Richmond Riverside is indeed no more than a series of facades, with parking space underneath, and open-plan offices, aluminium windows and air-conditioning inside: 'False Georgian architecture', writes Peter Blundell Jones,[203] 'devalues real architecture as inevitably as forged notes devalue normal currency,' and concludes that the architect's role has here been reduced to that of decorator.

Similarly, Zevi criticises Charles Moore's Piazza d'Italia (New Orleans) for mis-using well-known symbols and archetypes, and for being content 'to play around with them, renouncing planning for scenography and cosmetics, without rediscovering the real workings of things'.[204] To call the Piazza d'Italia dismissively a version of Disneyland, with all Disneyland's insubstantiality, may well be accurate; but then Moore himself sees that complex as no less than the apotheosis of the American Dream.[205] The Piazza d'Italia is avowedly playful, so to compare it with the Parthenon would scarcely be fair: but is there some message here about the marginality of Classicism, about the new uses of the past in a continent creating its own traditions by destroying European ones? Perhaps, but what grates on the purists is the purposeful misuse of architectural elements within a tinsel, theatrical setting – the transplanted mangling of European traditions which jar in a country where both native traditions and transmuted classical ones grow strong. As Klotz notes,[206] 'Some column capitals are reminiscent of crystalline Art Deco brooches, other capitals are ringed by neon necklaces.' He then suggests that 'these things tie the vocabulary of classical architecture to the present' – fortunately only partly true, and that surely at a level of ultimate superficiality, namely that of Las Vegas and Disneyland, where meaning is stripped from form, and iconography is thereby debased. Perhaps a more suitable comparison than the Parthenon is Arata Isozaki's Civic Centre in Tsukuba (1980-3): the references here, from Michelangelo to Aldo Rossi, are much more sophisticated because they re-interpret the past, in the manner of Ledoux, rather than merely quoting from it.

Such a rigid attitude to Classicism as Quinlan Terry's would probably have mystified any of those previous generations of European architects – including Vitruvius and Ledoux – who looked so assiduously to the buildings of Rome or the Hellenistic East rather than to those of classical Greece. Only Alberti appears squeamish about how to deal correctly with pillars, columns arches and architraves. And therefore, from the post and beam standpoint, most European 'classicising' architecture of all ages is indeed a sham, dedicated at least partly to facade decoration, and to variations on a limited number of set themes, as has long been recognised. It may be characteristic of Post-Modernism that a landmark in its history was the 1980 Venice Biennale, which was precisely a display of facades – of cardboard-like cut-outs. But a facade is simply that: it is not a building, and cannot on its own carry meaning: as Porphyrios remarks[207] of Post-Modernism, 'by trenching on the properties of other branches like scenography and graphics, it lost sight of tectonics, architecture's distinguishing feature.' Is this why we see so few photographs of post-modern interiors?

The astringent criticism Post-Modernism attracts[208] is but

PHILIP JOHNSON AND JOHN BURGEE, AT & T BUILDING, NEW YORK CITY, 1978-1982

the other face of the rhetoric in which its proponents indulge; and if this generates more heat than light, at least it demonstrates that Classicism is still (or, perhaps, once more) an issue of burning interest – to the public no less than to the architectural profession. Thus it is ironic that we should find an architectural historian lamenting that the very study of the past 'has not served to enlarge the architect's perception … it has prompted [him] to make a number of adaptations of the most limited and limiting kind. [Architects] are composing with fragmentary rubbish.'[209]

Post-Modernism (or ornamentalism) certainly is a form of historicism, but it must be underlined that the actual use made by many post-modernists of ornament – whether classical in derivation or not – is often quite deliberately in opposition to its original usage. That is, ornament in the past was always applied to complement structure, not only in nature but also in proportion. There is no question in a Greek building, or in the majority of post-antique revivalist ones, of abusing the system of proportions, or applying motifs in areas for which they were not traditionally intended: indeed, one might say that ornament is locked into structure. Mannerism provides a very few exceptions, but it is important to remember that the most 'liberated' of all the classicists, namely Claude-Nicholas Ledoux, never abused proportionality.

For some post-modernists, however, the past becomes one vast storehouse of motifs ripe for the picking, and for application in situations where – to traditional eyes at least – they simply do not fit. Frequently this can lead to a tinsel-town, cut-out architecture, high in eye-appeal but low in substance. Of course, we might view some of this behaviour as similar to that of naughty children who need to shock – which is perhaps one of the motivations behind Johnson's AT&T Tower. And after all, a shock is better than blandness and boredom. Perhaps, therefore, one litmus-paper test for modernists and post-modernists is their attitude to ornamentation and its relationship (or lack of it) to structure.

Of course, the disjuncture between structure and decoration[210] is nothing new. Claude Bragdon, writing in 1917 of American architecture, notes that 'The mendacity of the Renaissance spirit has long been recognised,' and deplores its contemporary influence: 'The construction has been shaped by the living hand of necessity, and is therefore rational and logical; the outward expression is the result of the architect's "digging in the graveyard". There has been laid upon it the dead hand of the past. Free of this incubus, the engineer has succeeded; subject to it, the architect has failed.'[211]

But are straight imitations of past works – pastiches – really an essential part of all Post-Modernism? Should we, for example, expect 20th-century frescoes actually to look like their sources[212] and then laud such productions as the continuation of a a vital tradition? Or should we see them as kitsch – as exceptions in a movement which has more substantial achievements to offer? Does Carlo Maria Mariani's *It is forbidden to awake the gods* (Priv coll, 1984) make any contribution to art in this century or, rather, does not the past 'become a form of archaeological resuscitation'.[213] As a recent reviewer notes of the material exposed in Charles Jencks' *Post-Modernism: the New Classicism in Art and Architecture* (London 1988), 'This is Woolworth's Classicism … We really ought not to pay any more attention to this bland, soap-stone substitute for the real thing than we do to the mantlepiece trinkets tourists purchase on the stalls which cluster close to the Parthenon.'[214] Similarly some literary critics, such as Charles Newman, believe that the term Post-Modernism 'inevitably calls to mind a band of vainglorious contemporary artists following the circus elephants of Modernism with snow shovels;'[215] which captures the contentious, not to say confusing, flavour of the new movement. Again, according to one critic Post-Modernism, with its 'colourful, image-laden, neo-decorative extravagance', was popular because it 'recaptured a public eye that had grown weary of the bland, cold products of late modernist architecture, and have been prohibited by modernist dogma from taking any real pleasure in historical architecture.'[216]

If the argument between moderns and post-moderns is about the very nature of architecture, who is right? The intricacy of the problem stems from the speed of 20th-century development, from the upsurge of city-dwelling population, and not least from the need to rebuild as cheaply and as quickly as possible after devastating wars, generally in a manner encumbered – rather than liberated – by diverse theories about the social role of architecture. The kind of cityscape to which historically-minded architects turn their attention is necessarily radically different from ours, not only because it typically serves a much smaller population (unencumbered by industry or machines, especially vehicles), but also because it has evolved over centuries. Perhaps there are some bad Renaissance buildings; but one reason why there are proportionally more bad 20th-century buildings is because Time, the great reaper, has not yet applied to them that 'natural selection' which can separate the good from the ugly. After the mass-construction mistakes of the postwar period,[217] the best architects of our age – whether they are called post-modern or not – recognise the complexity of producing architecture today. Venturi, for example, rejects what he calls the false simplicity of much modernist architecture, and looks to the past for pointers toward solutions 'to the growing complexities of our functional problems.'[218] Philip Johnson's career echoes the development of architecture since the 1920s: he was once a *propaganda bureau* for the Hitchcock & Johnson book on *The International Style;* he designed work in the tradition of Mies, and demonstrated his clear grasp of the importance of the classical tradition *and* the contemporary context by declaring that 'Schinkel's work is unthinkable without a consideration of Ledoux, Boullée and Gilly, Mies without Picasso, Mondrian, Lissitzky'; but during the 1950s he became increasingly dissatisfied with the straight lines and geometric shapes of the International Style, blossoming into what he calls a functional eclectic.[219]

Perhaps it is not only architecture, but society, which has become more complex in our century – too complex, that is, for the old solutions to work. Venturi's argument, like that of Johnson, is therefore not really against simplicity or Classicism, but against the dishonest hiding of complexity within a bland skin of simplicity: 'In Modern architecture we have operated too long under the restrictions of unbending rectangular forms supposed to have grown out of the technical requirements of the frame and the mass-produced curtain wall'[220] – although his interest in Mannerism (itself a wilful perversion of Classicism) is reflected in his own work.

Conceivably, what seems lacking to some in Modernism is not merely an aesthetic but also a spiritual dimension. Recalling Joan Evans' evocation of the symbolism and synthesis that is a hallmark of the medieval artistic achievement, Peter Fuller suggests that 'Modernism will only appear to be the legitimate and inevitable style of our century if we have entirely relinquished that sense of spiritual belonging and ultimate unity.'[221] The historicism of some post-moderns, forging links with the past, responds to these traditional needs, as does the classical tradition itself. As Philip Johnson remarks[222] of architecture today, 'strict-Classicism, strict-Modernism, and all shades in between, are equally valid. No generally persuasive "-ism" has appeared. It may be none will arise unless there is a worldwide, new religion or set of beliefs out of which an aesthetic could be formed.'

## Post-Modernism and Historicism

Just as with 19th-century architecture, one of the main debates about Post-Modernism revolves around the importance of historicism, and the nature of the sources to be used. In Paolo Portoghesi's words:

> The focus is on the presence of the past. The most practical modification is the approach to history. It permits the use of traditional forms without nostalgia or traditional reaction . . . [Post-Modernism] must be related to history like a door through which one can communicate. Architecture is based on conventions which are meaningless without a connection to the past.[223]

Yes – and our connections today are with Mies rather than with Michelangelo. The crux of the matter is what one actually does with the past, and what the product means – not with the fact that one re-uses it, which everyone must in some measure. Revivalism in any previous century has often been moderated by the sense of elapsed time, of change: Greek, Hellenistic and Roman architecture recapitulated, just as Renaissance and 17th-century work did, but each phase was recognisably distinct from its sources – a re-interpretation. There is one Parthenon, one Didymaion, one Pantheon and one Hagia Sophia. The Didymaion is no more a copy of the Parthenon than Hagia Sophia is of the Pantheon; and the Sultan Ahmet Mosque in Istanbul, the sources of which lie in both the Pantheon and Hagia Sophia, is a copy, much less a pastiche, of neither. Venturi's attitude to the past seems just right: 'When we re-examine – or discover – this or that aspect of earlier building production today, it is with no idea of repeating its forms, but rather in the expectation of feeding more amply new sensibilities that are wholly the product of the present'[224] – which is what pastiche cannot do.

Unfortunately, however, to tread the historicist path is frequently to indulge in what many view as pastiche, of which Post-Modernism provides plentiful examples – and not just of conventionally classicising buildings: compare Michael Graves' Benacerraf House addition of 1969 at Princeton[225] and his Hauselmann House (Fort Wayne 1967-8), which are very much in the Le Corbusier mould: 'Jencks calls them a futile, precarious poetic distortion of a Cubist syntax.'[226] For in Zevi's opinion Post-Modernism is:

> a futile, precarious phenomenon, lacking any cultural substance . . . I distinguish two contradictory trends in it. One is 'neo-academic'. It tries to copy Classicism and it is repressive, trying not to revitalise true classical canons, but rather 'classicist' design, such as the Ecole des Beaux-Arts. I would call it Napoleonic, fascist . . . The other tendency is antithetical: evasive, anarchic, saying

essentially 'do anything you like'. Its roots are in America's desire to break free from Europe's cultural patrimony[227]

In some circles, few more weighty insults could be found than to call something 'Beaux-Arts';[228] in others, European snootiness about American *faux pas* knows no bounds.

Balanced complaints about the noxious effects of historicism are of course much older than reactions to Post-Modernism. Thus Louis Sullivan (whose training at the Ecole des Beaux-Arts must have taught him much on the matter), speaking to the Chicago Architectural Club in 1899, said: 'a fraudulant and surreptitious use of historical documents, however suavely presented, however cleverly plagiarised, however neatly packed, however shrewdly intrigued, will constitute and will be held to be a betrayal of trusy'[229] – betrayal that is, of the architect's mission 'to express the life of your own day and generation'; whereas Sullivan perceived that 'the American architecture of today is the offspring of an illegitimate commerce with the mongrel styles of the past', and such imitation 'is a procedure unworthy of a free people'.[230] Half a century later, Bruno Zevi makes the same point, albeit without the understandable nationalism of Sullivan:

> to show that the vitality of today's architectural language is one with the task of interpreting history in a modern, almost futuristic version, so as to make it act effectively as an incentive to creativity. The passive imitation that went with revivalism and the indifference of some avantguardists toward history are both deplorable and absurd.[231]

Both comments point to a way of deciding the integrity of a work of art or architecture of any period which purports to be within the classical tradition: granted that the motifs are present, what does their use actually mean for contemporaries? If nothing or little, then the shadow of Classicism is present without the substance: the work of Mies, Sullivan and Lutyens passes the test; but much post-modernist work, in whatever medium, fails it.

Sullivan's genius made sure he was an exception to the general rule of the age, which was to be violently for or against revivalism or Modernism. The example of the American architect Ralph Adams Cram, a prolific designer of churches and university buildings in the first decades of this century, usually in a modified Gothic style (as in his Chapel for Princeton University, of 1929), will suffice. Reproduction was out: 'Consistent adherence to architectural styles that have a limited variety of form and details as in the Classical orders

or to 'authenticity' implying reproduction, is destructive to creative architecture.' Home, school and church are the three main inspirations of the architect, and their example can provide inspiration because they 'possess an unbroken continuity and sequence back through the Renaissance, Rome, Greece, even to Egypt' – but in the Cram style there can be no Modernism; '"Modernism", as it is understood today being that unhistoric and arbitrary style of design emanating from France and Germany.'[232] With such delicious xenophobia does Cram express the love of the familiar and the fear of the new.

It is not as easy to recognise a post-modernist as it is a modernist building; or, differently put, there is a much greater variety of styles today than during the reign of the modern movement – a feature which derives only partly from Post-Modernism's inherent historicism. The movement – it is no less than that – delineates an attitude toward the purpose of architecture in society, but shelters a range of styles so bewildering as to defie the categorising yearnings of all but Charles Jencks. The post-modernist ethos toward the built environment is well encapsulated by Robert Venturi, whose approach depends on the exigencies of the commission: as he says: 'Our scheme for the FDR memorial was architecture and landscape; our fountain for the Philadelphia Fairmount Park Commission, was architecture and sculpture; our design for Copley Plaza, architecture and urban design . . .'[233] – that is, a sensitivity to environment heightened by his study of the classicising past. In this sense only, perhaps, is he against the ethos of some 'modern' architecture, which ignores the environment by producing buildings that may look like updated Greek temples but which, unlike Greek architecture, are insensitive to their surroundings.

Whether post-modernists are as careful of the setting as they would have us believe depends on one's point of view; and the sensitive/insensitive dichotomy can be illustrated by Michael Graves' Portland Public Service Building, in Oregon, designed in 1980. Intended to sit between the classical City Hall and the equally classical County Courthouse, it certainly has some classical features itself, but towers above its neighbours rather like a version of Battersea Power Station designed by Ledoux.[234] The main features of the 18th-century *architecture parlante* are there in the original design and model – the Orders stripped down to ciphers, the focus on an few features (the gigantic keystone), the sculpture, and the monumentality (this last emphasised by the tiny acropolis of buildings on the flat roof). But what really marks it out is its

MICHAEL GRAVES, PORTLAND PUBLIC SERVICE BUILDING, PORTLAND, OREGON, 1980-83

megalomania – delusions of grandeur on a scale that Ledoux kept carefully in his drawings, but did not use in his executed work. The Portland Building is certainly impressive, and clearly classical in motif and general form; but it does not sit comfortably within its environment, for its motifs are hugely mis-scaled, deafening with its vulgarity and high colouring its more reticent neighbours. Indeed, the local chapter of the American Institute of Architects, in a spirited opposition to the design, suggested that it should have been built in Las Vegas. In fact, comparing model with finished building, the result is considerably more staid in decoration, and less highly coloured; and the cranky temples on the roof have been omitted. Given an india-rubber of the same scale as the building, it might even be possible to erase some of the offending post-modernist elements, revealing the unremarkable block beneath. Other post-modernists, however, respect both the vocabulary of and the proportioning of Classicism, albeit in the 'free-form' variety of Palladio and Ledoux. Moore, Grover & Harpers Samnis Hall (Cold Spring Harbour, 1978-81) looks like an updating out of Ledoux of a villa by Palladio, both in plan and elevation. Nevertheless, it also looks up-to-date, not only in its use of low cost materials (although Palladio did likewise in many of his brick and stucco villas), but also in its subdued colouring and post-modern cardboard-cutouts, as in the serliana in the entry hall. This is indeed updated Classicism, still inspired by a tradition which it is helping to change, and not to ossify. And if one wants to study the influence of Ledoux on our century, one can do worse than study Asplund's Stockholm City Library (1920–8), or indeed the work of Adolf Loos. Ledoux was therefore well known to the moderns, and is not a rediscovery of the post-moderns!

Much controversy has also been generated by Philip Johnson's AT&T Tower, designed in 1977. The 'middle' of this building is traditional skyscraper; but the 'podium' is formed by an elegant version of the serliana, while the top has a sloping, broken pediment reminiscent of a Chippendale bookcase. Certainly, the whole design is a slap in the face for traditional Modernism; and 20 years ago, its inflation of standard motifs to gigantic size would have seemed a joke. Today, because everything can be made to slot into place when provided with a historical context, we can place the AT&T firmly in the tradition of sykscrapers such as the Empire State or the Chrysler Building, even if for some the pedimental motif is hard to swallow.

New York may be a city where – architecturally – anything goes. London is not, and the lively public interest over the National Gallery extension must be seen against the traditional scenario of wicked developers who rape the environment, thereby destroying the national heritage. The debate was peculiarly well focused because the competition was for an extension to fit in not only with Trafalgar Square itself, but especially with William Wilkins' existing National Gallery, beloved of all visitors and Londoners, and a work of flawed Classicism. Had the problem – opportunity? – occurred in Paris, perhaps the French would have pulled it down and started again, on the principle of Les Halles! Many competitors felt bound to use classical forms and motifs[235] especially reminiscences or echoes of Neo-Classicism. Campbell, Zogolovitch, Wilkinson & Gough provided a serliana for an entrance and, inside, a loggia, and a square segmented dome on the Soane model at Lincoln's Inn Fields. Henry N. Cobb (I M Pei & Partners) has a rotunda for the entrance, while Jeremy Dixon & BDP quote the Tower of the Winds for their main entrance. Venturi's design is much more subdued, but it is still recognisably classical, matching the Wilkins' facade.

Another London project which has received a lot of attention is Stirling, Wilford & Associates' Clore Gallery for the Turner Collection, at the Tate Gallery, of 1982-5. The starting point was similar to that at the National Gallery – namely another much-loved Neo-classical structure with which the extension had to live. Given the special problems involved in designing a good gallery, Stirling was especially favoured for the task, following the success and publicity attending his monumental and exciting Staatsgalerie in Stuttgart (1977-84), with its updating of traditional motifs, and reliance upon sweeping, elemental shapes. His solution for the Clore Gallery is Classicism in the modern manner: calm and low, with diocletian window set in blank masonry, a monumental entrance setting like something from a pre-Hellenic tomb, and insistent geometric wall patterning. What a change of style from the rough and uncompromising Engineering Building (of 1959-63) for Leicester University!

Public buildings are, of course, a very different matter from private dwellings, a genre which suits Post-Modernism very well: here, in contradistinction to the gravity of civic architecture (at least from a classical standpoint), playfulness and lighthearted pastiche are part of a tradition – and so is breaking the rules, as Andrea Palladio's work demonstrates. Indeed, it is arguable that much architecture – classicising architecture in particular – is far too solemn, and takes itself far too seriously. Classicising architecture, with its undeni-

VENTURI, SCOTT BROWN & ASSOCIATES, EXTENSION TO THE NATIONAL GALLERY, PERSPECTIVE, 1987

able overtones of high, improving art, rectitude and social betterment, might seem intended to overawe people – the extreme (and almost Baroque) overstatement of the same idea in Ledoux' or Boullée's unbuilt creations, where humankind is immeasurably small against the grandeur of the construction. Perhaps public architecture should be approachable (after all, we all make up part of the public) so that, to take one glaring example, museum and gallery architecture should entice rather than distance its customers – a decided plus for the post-modernists, with their re-use of familiar forms and motifs. After the rarified perfection of Modernism, post-modernists are again practising populism in architecture, many of them inspired by Robert Venturi's *Complexity and Contradiction*.

The villa ideal, from Pliny through to the Renaissance and 18th-century Europe, continues in our own age, whereas its bigger brothers – grand country houses – were blotted out by the age of the common man. Just as for Le Corbusier, Mies or Philip Johnson, wealthy patrons help. A good example of the robustness of Palladio's ideas and syntax is Stanley Tigerman's Villa Proeh (Highland Park, Illinois, 1979-80);[236] while Robert Venturi's 'My Mother's House' (Chestnut Hill, Pennsylvania, 1962), might stand as the most important

exemplar of a sensitive re-use of the past rather than a supine submission to it. He has re-thought the traditional usage of architectural vocabulary, and rendered it down, as it were, into spare and sometimes playful motifs. The boldness of the saddle roof and the split gable succeed, perhaps, because they are backed up by firm, three-dimensional (even block-like, Ledoux-like) design. The same can be said of the vestigial 'arched porch' over the square, undetailed entrance, which is little more than a curved string-course; or indeed of the meeting of the skylight and the saddle roof at the rear of the house to form a Palladian window.[237] Playful some of this may be; but it is more than mere facadism not only because old motifs are re-worked with wit (rather than simply cut out of a copy of Banister Fletcher), but because it is designed as a set of volumes, not stage-sets. This is, in sum, a reworking of Classicism as refreshing – and startling – as was that of Ledoux himself. The same applies to his unbuilt project of 1962, of a house for Millard Meiss, the art historian[238] which does honour to the (Palladian) past with wit and imagination, but does not copy it.

Perhaps one doesn't always need to think deeply about the past to produce satisfying architecture; but Venturi has done so, and surely it has helped in his case, for the result is both

STIRLING WILFORD & ASSOCIATES, CLORE GALLERY, LONDON, 1982-86

stable and dramatic, simple and complex. If one were to retort that the product cannot be classical because of all the rules that have been broken – windows 'hanging' from a string-course on the facade; the split pediment; the 'naked' entrance – then the response is that Classicism (as this book has tried to show) is a developing, changing phenomenon, with rules that can be broken as long as the basic ethos of balance and harmony result. In this fine building, Venturi demonstrates the difference between rigid adherence to the past, and a spirited re-use of it. But as with Mies and his followers, so with Venturi's imitators; if the work of Mies spawned face-less, anonymous clones, then Venturi's influential writings gave rise to an attitude of cultural populism or 'main street' style, this in its turn being 'little more than a manipulative form of admass advocacy and giving rise to populist collage', as well as to cannibalised forms of eclectic historicism.[239] However, between civic buildings and single-owner dwell-ings lie apartment blocks – an important element in Post-Modernism because this is one area where it is felt Modern-ism went badly wrong. Ricardo Bofill's Palace of Abraxas at Marne-la-Vallee, begun in 1978, shows a similar gigantism to Graves' Portland Building, by the inflation of familiar clas-sical elements such as columns and pediments. The great

podium, with its light rustication, is strongly reminiscent of 18th-century French architecture (as is his La Place du Nombre d'Or at Montpellier, of 1978-84), but the 'super-structure' quite deliberately misuses the motifs of Classicism by inflating them laterally (the pediments) or stretching them vertically (the pilasters on the facade of the two wings) so that they look awkward and unbalanced. For one whose sympa-thies lie with traditional classical balance and moderation, the building has a Lego-brick appearance, as if built by a giant without taste. Even the podium, for all its supposed pedigree, is unconvincing, because reminiscence is very different from invention. We live in the 20th century, not the 17th or 18th.

Bofill's Les Arcades du Lac (St-Quentin-en-Yvelines, 1974-80), is more classical in its proportions, with its use of a giant order and an imposing attic topped by a make-believe balustrade. Its sources are clear: Bernini's designs for the re-building of the Louvre for the plan, and Versailles for the elevation, laced with a little traditional arcading for the central circular space. This might well be a Versailles for the people (or at least for the middle-class); but do we really need pastiches of 17th-century architecture at the end of the 20th century? If pastiche there must be, why choose Jules-Har-douin, with all his italianate bombast (which Bernini would have loved), when the better – and much more French – Classicism of François Mansart was available? The answer might be that reticence is not a quality which sits well with much Post-Modernism. Indeed, if a stylistic term must be applied to either Les Arcades du Lac, or to the Palace of Abraxas, then it must be baroque – an inflation of post-antique Classicism, although frequently finding chapter and verse for its extravagances in Hellenistic antiquity.[240] Toy building blocks, in the sense of vestigially classical motifs rendered down into eternally classical shapes like the cube and the cylinder, do not necessarily make bad architecture, as the example of Ledoux makes clear. Takefumi Aida's Toy Block House III (1980-81), in Tokyo, updates Ledoux by drawing inspiration both from abstraction in general, and from the traditions of 20th-century Classicism. This work differs from the approach of Bofill or Graves in that a strict feeling for the traditional proportions between the elements is retained: Aida, like Ledoux, designs in three dimensions, and the resulting block-like quality is not only pleasing in itself, but provides an antidote to facadism. If Post-Modernism does indeed have to come to terms with industrialisation (and socially-minded architects recognise that it must), then Aida's work proves that this can be achieved without sacrificing a true attachment to the traditions of the past – although his recent Kazawa residence in Tokyo has been castigated as belonging to 'the new generation of Collage Architecture – a classic symptom of Japan's chronic lack of a unifying architectural language'[241]

An interesting characteristic of Post-Modernism, perhaps derived from its proclaimed attachment to Classicism, is its desire to be an orthodoxy, the True Way of architecture. This is probably to be expected, in that many exciting movements that break away from the norms end up by imposing their own. It is certainly consistent with the 'moral' view of the classical tradition, and with Post-Modernism's desire to play a political and social role[242] – a desire heightened by what are seen as the mistakes of Modernism: as Aldo Rossi writes, 'I believe that my revolt and my protest against the Modern Movement were also born of political and ideological assumptions.'[243] Rossi is certainly sincere; but to many the architecture resulting from such assertions can be hollow,[244] for they believe Post-Modernism lacks both honesty and integrity, while impugning much of modern architecture for the lack of precisely the same virtues. In short, there is a clear attempt by post-modernists to ensure that their work has a pedigree – that it is not some minor tributary, but integrated in the very mainstream of art.[245]

Another characteristic of post-modernist criticism is surely a tendency to over-analysis and partition, conspicuous in the writings of Charles Jencks, 'who derives an almost sensuous pleasure in categorisation'.[246] Placing things in categories is, of course, a usual pursuit of historians; but a glance at any of Jencks' works will show that there are very few contemporary productions which do not somehow get under the umbrella of Post-Modernism, or Classicism, in some guise. The latest book, for instance (*Post-Modernism: the New Classicism in Art and Architecture*), has chapters on metaphysical, narrative, allegorical, realist, revivalist, urbanist and eclectic Classicism; but, bewilderingly, it is the last chapter – not the first! – which deals with *The Emergent Rules*. Such a broad church of definitions recalls the old refrain, 'When everybody's somebody, then no-one's anybody'. This is not wholly Jencks' fault, of course, for the very phenomenon of Post-Modernism is confusing and frequently contradictory.[247] Such *ad hominem* remarks are inevitable, given the nature of the post-modernist debate, which frequently gives an impression of fabrication rather than natural growth.

More seriously, however (in view of their stated interests), few attempts seem to be made by the post-modernists to come firmly to grips with the past, with the result that a new edifice is erected on foundations that misinterpret the truth, and statements that are blatantly false go unqueried. When Jencks writes that 'Modernism cut architectural expression off from the past'[248] by producing buildings not 'rooted in place and time', this is demonstrably untrue, as a glance at the work of Mies should convince. And if the best examples he can find of Post-Modernism's supplying 'a public discourse worthy of our time'[249] – an ironically sybilline statement – then it is a pity that attention is not focused on works of higher quality than Bofill's Arcades du Lac or Moore's Piazza d'Italia. The best weapon against the supposed iniquities of Modernism is good architecture, not dubious interpretations of the past.

We might therefore add yet another characteristic to much post-modern discourse in architecture: while 'the sources' are often displayed like totems alongside photographs of the new work, there seems to be a disinclination to discuss quality. Obeisance is now made to Ledoux rather than to Mies, but the fact that neither actually copied the past is forgotten. As Demetri Porphyrios comments, 'contemporary architecture bathes in the pantheistic limbo of eclecticism . . . leafs through history caricaturing remembrances and attempts to capture the illusion of culture cheaply'.[280] Con-

RICARDO BOFILL AND TALLER DE ARCHITECTURA, PALACE OF ABRAXAS, MARNE LE VALLEE, FRANCE, 1978-83

versely Porphyrios sees Classicism – quite correctly, in accord with its millenial traditions – as a matter of 'sacramental power . . . over contingent life and nature'.

Post-Modernism's proclaimed critique of Modernism and attachment to tradition would be devastating were they true, because they would call into question the direction of a whole movement. Certainly, there are post-modernists who eschew any visible connection with 'modern' architects – such as Ricardo Bofill with his 1980-84 apartment complex at Marne-a-Vallée in France, with its decidedly mannerist mis-use of the Orders – but there are others, like Richard Meier, who are clearly inspired by elements from Le Corbusier and the beginnings of Modernism, as in his Atheneum at New Harmony, Indiana, of 1975-80: Meier is a very inventive architect, and the brilliant use he makes of his sources helps demonstrate that Modernism did not kill off Classicism, but simply generated a different version of it. Of course, doctrinaire viewpoints are bound to see doctrine in the works on which they focus; but we should recognise that Modernism is far from being monolithic: for all the purism of Mies van der Rohe, what about the multiplicity of Le Corbusier, of his Ronchamp Chapel (1950-4) as opposed to the monumental Court of Justice at Chandigarh, of 1956? Or consider some of

his villas, with their demonstrable inspiration (which does not amount to pastiche) from Palladio.

One problem, however, is peculiar to architecture:[251] is Post-Modernism really a style conceived for and suited to our populist (and some would say post–bourgeois) age? Or is much of its preciosity – castigated by, for example, Tafuri[252] – so expensive as to remove it completely from any kind of social relevance? Is post-modernist architecture for the rich, like traditional Italian villas or English country houses, or is it for all of us? Or did the Romans think much the same about those nouveau-riche villas at Pompeii? After all, one of the characteristics of traditional Classicism is precisely that it is not populist[253] – whereas one positive step Post-Modernism has certainly taken is to bring architecture to the people by providing motifs with which they can identify, either through contemporary cultural signals, or by evocation of historicist ones. Certainly, many post-modernists accept and rejoice in the use of standard catalogue components where possible; so that, in terms of cost, the post-modern variety of Classicism can indeed be made to work in the age of the masses. Hence the old 19th-century opposition between classical=cheap (because devoid of decoration) and Gothic=expensive (because decorated) breaks down, in spite of the post-modern

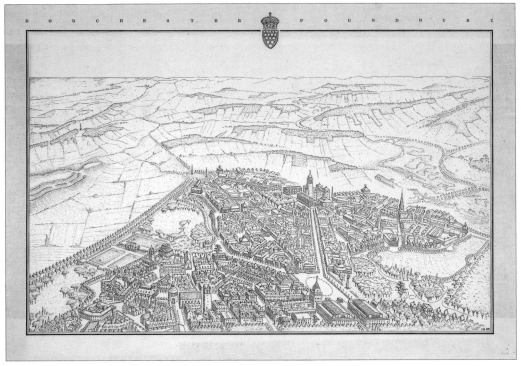

LEON KRIER, POUNDBURY PARK, DORCHESTER, 1989

inclination toward ornament. Is this just pop culture, or a solid re-evaluation of Classicism? An example to illustrate the problem would be Venturi's unbuilt project of 1979 for a country house incorporating a Palladian window based on one at George Washington's house at Mount Vernon, of 1776; for Hersey,[254] what Venturi has done is to 'turn provincial solecisms into savage virtues' – a procedure which would have been pointless had not the source been so well known. Perhaps, then, historicist architecture can only work well when the source *is* recognisable, as with Allan Greenberg's Mount Vernon-based house in Connecticut.[255]

**Conclusion: Classicism, Post-Modernism and the Future**
As we have seen, the classical tradition has changed radically over the centuries, and it is change that has kept it alive and relevant. With the modern/post-modern debate and the polarisation of positions that it apparently entails, it is important to keep in mind that there are few true absolutes involved. Modernism itself was – is – far from a dogma; and we have seen the etymological contortions needed to impose some kind of order on the very concept of Post-Modernism. Architects themselves develop through time – the work of James Stirling being a good example – so that it is likely that Post-

Modernism as perceived today will turn out to be but another transient *ism* in a century addicted (and curiously so, if this is the century of the individual) to the very idea of movements. Unfortunately, commentators have obscured rather than clarified the matter by attempts at categorisation – a process extended by a tendency to view Post-Modernism as coming after Modernism rather than existing alongside it, so that all contemporary buildings would be by such a definition postmodern.

To an historian, what is surprising about the post-modernist episode is the concomitant re-evaluation of Classicism as an issue for impassioned debate – surprising after the stultification it endured for much of the 19th century. But what of the future? Will *Classicism* survive the post-modernist onslaught and emerge with sufficient coherence to serve future generations? Or is this terminology now no more than a lax way of referring to the accumulated storehouse of 'traditional' art and architecture? Is the current vogue for classicising citation a superficial whim, or just a version of all art's need to link somehow to the past? To pose the question in another way, are modern 'classical' works in various media still part of a continuing tradition, as some scholars maintain,[256] or isolated historicist pastiches marginalised by other,

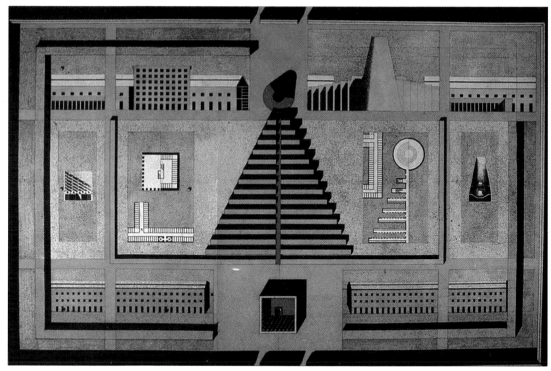

ALDO ROSSI, MODENA CEMETERY, 1975

stronger movements?

To extend the question, how many modern instances of Classicism have that same firm base of social and philosophical acceptance which we have seen to be essential to the longevity of the tradition itself? How many, using William Porter's neat definition of architecture, make the connection between technology and culture? The answer must be few: some post-modernist works are pastiches, not recreations; and they are hollow precisely because they lack substantial ideas to reinforce their forms; consequently, their forms lack strength and conviction. True classicising art is programmatic, not incidental.

Perhaps the value and hence the potential longevity of Post-Modernism will depend on its relative balance of tradition against innovation. Unfortunately, attempts to demonstrate a continuity of Classicism, in the sense of adherence to both the forms and the ideas of Greece or Rome, are often frustrated, because unless practitioners indulge in mere decorative pastiche, or facadism,[257] the links with the classical tradition can be hard to discern, even if optimism prevails – as in the recently expressed belief in the continuing validity of the *envois* of the *Prix de Rome*.[258]

Fortunately, however, Post-Modernism is not the only ve-hicle today for the salvation of Classicism. Indeed, many 20th-century architects have been inspired and extended by the past without being crippled by quoting from it; so that we can understand the attraction of the layout of Villa Adriana for Louis Kahn, or specifically of the lighting arrangements of the Canopus at the same site for Le Corbusier, without expecting them to produce historicist buildings from such studies.[259] Denys Lasdun perhaps views the value of the classical past in a similar light. In his Royal Gold Medal address he spoke as follows:

> I suppose all those ideas [in his work] return to the perennial lessons of Greece. There is an attempt somewhere to recapture in some small way that exquisite reciprocal relationship which they achieved between geometrical form, siting and spirit of place – a sense of belonging to time, place and people and being at home in the world.[260]

Certainly, then, there are classical traditions outside Post-Modernism, which have either survived the onslaught of Modernism or, from a different perspective, contributed to Modernism's own development. Classicism, that is, far from being a tradition avoided by Modernism, has itself been modified by it. This point will bear repetition precisely be-

ALLAN GREENBERG, OFFICES FOR BRENT PUBLICATIONS, NEW YORK, 1985

cause of the claims of the post-modernists about the rupture between Modernism and the past – a rupture which, they claim, invalidates Modernism itself. Once this claim is dismissed, both Modernism and Post-Modernism can be seen to draw on the past. Bruno Zevi's aim of showing 'that the vitality of today's architectural language is one with the task of interpreting history in a modern, almost futuristic version' can surely stand for all the arts, as can Philip Johnson's off-the-cuff comment, which apparently distresses Charles Jencks (who exposes some of his Johnson's as at least crypto-fascist!): 'My direction is clear; eclectic tradition. This is not academic revivalism. There are no Classic orders or Gothic finials. I try to pick up what I like throughout history. We cannot not know history.'[261]

One characteristic which unites Modernism and Post-Modernism to Classicism is the ease with which they have variously swept the world over the last few centuries. This may be due (as it arguably was in the Greek and Roman world) more to political and technological causes rather than to artistic ones; and, likewise, the current reactions to such cultural imperialism are political as much as artistic. 'It should not be a revelation to anyone', writes Brian Brace Taylor,[262] 'that architecture is a means for communicating a set of values and a system of ideas, commonly called an ideology.' Hence the current interest in regionalism and architectural identity[263] leads many to see Classicism as a style imported for colonial purposes, and which has little to do with the values of the countries concerned. The qualification is for those cases where a European/local blend was demanded in order to make a political point, as with Herbert Baker's Secretariat & Council Hall at New Delhi (1920-27) in a mixture of classical and Mughal styles 'to epitomise the aims of mutual respect and tolerance among two rich cultural heritages desired by the British'.[264] But all this mongrelism (or facadism, to use a contemporary term) really does is to provide an inaccurate version of native traditions, which deserve more sympathetic handling. Curtis asks[265] 'what Classicism has to do with the search for an authentic Indian expression? After all it was Lutyens who sneered at the Indian architecture of the past as so many "Moghul and Hindu contraptions".'

The same view can also be held of Modernism and Post-Modernism: the motives and type of colonialism have changed, but the results of the process are usually the same. Architects in the Third World have therefore begun to turn their attention away from such imports and toward their own heritage, in order to re-discover architectural traditions that reflect their own ideology without necessarily being *retardataire:* a good example is Sumet Jumsai's design for the Bank of Asia Building in Bangkok, which is not only a modern high-rise with high-tech additions, but also a witty recapitulation of Thai Bhuddist temple forms. Whether such regionalism will prevail remains to be seen, for there are people with money in most Third World countries who identify with the West and its architecture – and who appreciate buildings such as Ong Ard's recent post-modernist high-rise apartment block in Bangkok. This is topped by a neo-classical temple, and decorated with pedimented windows and a Tower-of-the-Winds-like gazebo. Nor is this building an exception in Bangkok: Taylor suggests[266] that 'The rampant use of neo-classical fragments (Greek, Roman, and hybrid versions of these) in reinforced concrete to decorate buildings, is the result of a combination of factors: the architects' desire to be part of a "global" trend characterised by Western classical decoration and a certain strata of Thai society that wishes to advertise their worldly success.' The phenomenon is not restricted to Thailand: in India, for example, there are still Indian architects 'labouring under the undigested Western influence'.[267] When Charles Jencks refers to 'Post-Modern regionalism: the expression of place',[268] we might reasonably conclude that he is confused, seeing regionalism and the 'global village' mentality of Post-Modernism as symbiotic, whereas from a non-Western (or Westernised) perspective they are mutually exclusive. He is not the only one: Isozaki's Tsukuba Civic Centre is a distinguished composition, but what has his re-use of Michelangelo's Campidoglio motif got to do with Japan?

This brief excursion in the Third World underlines the continuing prestige of Classicism even in areas where it has no natural roots. Clients of the Roman Empire built in much the same way as some westernised Thais do today, and for the same range of cultural/political reasons. In ancient times, areas such as Britain and France (and indeed North Africa, Asia Minor and the Near East) received Classicism as part of the colonial package; and the post-medieval architectural history of Romanised Western Europe describes the slow re-assimilation of what were now viewed as venerable 'roots', mostly re-imported from Italy, the epicentre of the Renaissance. Today, it seems as if the triad of Modernism, Post-Modernism and Classicism will take over the whole world.

So Classicism is alive and well but, as always, living in interesting times. It is certainly strong and flexible enough to survive pastiche, facadism and general mis-use, and will die out only when the value system which it embodies has nothing left to offer. That is, when the infrastructure of Classicism has melted away, leaving only empty motifs, so that all that remains is Classicism as a style rather than as a tradition – an adherence to ideals of clarity, restraint and formal structure which are as attainable in painting and sculpture (whether abstract or figurative) as they are in architecture. As Max Radin has it:

> Tradition has social significance only when the old or the long established idea becomes something of value in the estimation of some or all of the members of a community and its age and origin is referred to only as an assurance of its value. It produces in a nation or in a group an exalted group consciousness and is therefore effective in creating groups or in re-establishing them. In all its aspects it retains enough of its primary characteristics of vagueness, remoteness of source and wide ramification to make it seem peculiarly strong to those who have recourse to it and peculiarly weak to those who mean to reject it.[269]

Whether the classical tradition dies may well depend upon whether the rest of the world eventually decides to retain European and American architectural ideas closely linked to European cultural history, or to develop architectural forms conceivably better suited to local history and traditions. As we saw at the beginning of this book, however, *Classicism* is also a term which can be used to refer to the best in any tradition, and thus help preserve that sense of difference which should continue to make the world a diversely interesting place. So perhaps we should hope for regional diversity in artistic and architectural ideas and forms, thereby avoiding both the facile 'native imagery' of airport art and the stultifying sameness of airport architecture.

———— * ————

ROBERT A M STERN ARCHITECTS, OBSERVATORY HILL DINING HALL, UNIVERSITY OF VIRGINIA, CHARLOTTESVILLE, 1982-4

## Epilogue

Until recently, Classicism was thought totally outdated, if only by certain sections of the profession, and certain critics and interested observers. As this book has established, however, far from being a concept which belongs exclusively to the past, Classicism once again holds an important place in the development of new architecture – of work which is exciting and innovative at least in part, because it is firmly founded in tradition.

This epilogue surveys briefly some of the current players in the game – a game which often has heated political and sociological overtones – by examining how they deal with the past. This will enable us to summarise the current position of Classicism by looking to the architects most responsible for furthering its cause. In contemporary architecture, the way forward for Classicism has taken several forms, illustrated by various groups of architects. And given its vitality and popularity, we cannot discount the possibility that other interpretations, equally inspired by the tradition, will appear in the years to come.

In its quest for traditional values Post-Modernism has often looked to Classicism both for justification and for inspiration. The result is exemplified first and foremost by the activities of American architects such as Graves, Venturi, Moore and Johnson, as already discussed. Arata Izosaki has also produced works in a similar idiom in Japan. In Britain the main exponent of the style has been Terry Farrell, whose Henley Regatta Headquarters or Clifton Nurseries, for example, draw on specific aspects of the classical language. British architect James Stirling also displays strong classical leanings in some of his work, especially in his monumental (if not austere) Neue Staatsgalerie in Stuttgart.

Post-Modern Classicism is controversial. By employing individual features (like pediment or column) without necessary reference to the incumbent canon of style accompanying it, it sometimes claims to take an ironic stance. This is felt by true disciples of Classicism to deprive it of its *gravitas* (or general seriousness). Playfulness is fine for some buildings, but seems to sit badly with a desired monumentality. What is more, many of Post-Modernism's 'excesses' can be viewed as the straightforward and wilful *mis-use* of classical features, as if one were trying to deal with a language when only elements of vocabulary were known, but no syntax. So that just as ignorance of the syntax of the English language would surely lead to a bad poem, so the ignorance or deliberate perversion of architectural syntax leads to bad buildings. Fundamentalist classicist Demetri Porphyrios has sharply criticised such a style, writing that 'the lessons to be learnt today from Classicism … are not to be found in Classicism's stylistic wrinkles but in Classicism's rationality'. Nevertheless, it is chastening to recall that correctness has but rarely been a feature of the classical tradition; so that what appears outrageous or silly today may well be accepted tomorrow.

Not all architects, however, part readily from the rationalism of the tradition, one of the features of which can be an insistent emphasis on essential geometry. This rationalism is found most prominently in the works of Aldo Rossi. For example, his cemetery at Modena, stripped down to the bare essentials, and therefore without any of that detailing which architects from the Renaissance until recently studied so intensely, yet retains the basic classical form. In a different and less radical way Ignacio Linazosoro in, for example, his Medical Centre at Segura, in Spain 1983-5, and Porphyrios himself also adopts a fundamentalist approach to Classicism. This makes their work more recognisable as part of the tradition – Rossi having clear ties with Italian architecture of the 1930s and 1940s, Porphyrios with the Greeks and the Greek tradition, and Linazosoro with aspects of International Modernism.

Neither Rossi nor Porphyrios 'excerpt' Classicism by plundering scissors-and-paste style the work of the past. But a few architects are indeed exponents of a more historicist line, with direct revivalist or canonic use of Classicism. Quinlan Terry's facadism at Richmond Riverside and the works of John Blatteau and Allan Greenberg are perhaps to be seen as part of a conscious aesthetic revivalism. Robert Adam combines a canonic approach with a keen interest in modern technology. At Dognerfield Park, for example, he justified the absence of glazing bars on the windows by the use of thoroughly climate-controlled technology. Nevertheless, this work might be more correctly described as Baroque than classical, for it has more than a whiff of Hawksmoor. By far the most pluralistic approach to Classicism is adopted by architects like Robert Stern or Ricardo Bofill. They have allowed classical ideals to interact with more modern vernaculars in the synthesis of an evolving style.

As always with Classicism, we should not ignore the strong foundation of theory, which continues to exert influence. Perhaps the most traditonal view of Classicism as a prescription for the environment has been taken by Leon Krier. His fundamentalism has gone further than most, in considering the urban environment as a unit, rather than following the deplorable tendency (so often seen) of having buildings do

DEMETRI PORPHYRIOS, HOUSE IN KENSINGTON, INTERIOR VIEW, 1987

violence to their setting: he reminds us that buildings cannot be considered separately from the environment in which they stand. Like his brother, Rob Krier, whose influential publications also expound the cause, Leon Krier's radical approach has amounted to an international crusade for the return to traditional planning values that take account of the urban setting. His plan for the redevelopment of Spitalfields Market area (1980) hoped to recreate a medieval street pattern, whilst his Master Plan for Washington DC evoked the full-blooded Romantic visions of the 19th century, still using a classical vocabulary.

At Seaside, Florida, Krier acted as consultant for architects Andres Duany and Elizabeth Plater-Zyberk. Here a new town development in an idiom appropriate to its setting, applies a wide variety of rationalised classical details within a strictly classical composition: Krier's *Belvedere*, for example, is inspired both by the antique and by the local clapperboard traditions. Most recently Leon Krier has had the opportunity to produce plans for the redevelopment of Poundbury Park in the Duchy of Cornwall for the Prince of Wales. This follows in the wake of the architectural debate fired by the Prince's recent comments and concerns about architecture – comments which have found supporters and detractors in almost equal measure. The project constitutes a major contribution to the search for a way forward for building that avoids the perceived pitfalls of Modernism, without having to resort to straightforward context-free historicism.

There are glorious precedents, of course, for princes interesting themselves in architecture (as for bishops concerning themselves with politics); and the debate, for all that it seems to generate more heat than light, has done nothing but good, because it has focused public opinion on at least some of the problems and options for preserving what integrity is left in our urban fabric, and developing that fabric with sensitivity.

There was a world-wide classical revival before his intervention, but it was at a specialised level. Now architecture – and classicising architecture at that – is a topical issue for the press and the media. Long may it remain so.

Indeed, it is exciting to see the millennial ideas and forms of Classicism exercising architects in the production of yet more fruitful variations, especially when their colleagues in painting, sculpture and the graphic arts view Classicism as but one source among a crowd of others. Although there are plenty of examples of Post-Modernism that antedate it, the Strada Novissima in the Venice 1980 Biennale is a landmark in the broader development of its popularity. But looking at real buildings (rather than at this academic demonstration), which *types* of Classicism will survive into the next century? That which builds in an 18th-century manner, as if nothing had happened in architecture between Robert Adam and Mies van der Rohe? That which keeps the framework of Classicism but strips away the detailing which might seem to age and date it? Facadism, where the Classicism is a skin-deep *jeu d'esprit* covering a building which is in all other respects truly 'modern'? Time will tell, but the fundamental Classicism of architects like Aldo Rossi and Arata Isozaki seems to this author to have logic, vigour and integrity on its side, as well as a pensive originality: it is new, but accepts tradition gracefully. Harold Macmillan once remarked that tradition doesn't mean that the living are dead, but rather that the dead are still alive. Similarly Richard Rogers, not noted for classicising buildings, nevertheless makes the same point from the other end of the telescope, reminding us that architecture thrives on innovation, not stagnation. Architecture is the reflection of the society that produces it; one must live with one's time, using new technologies while retailing a sense of harmony; without innovation, the masterpieces of the past would not exist.

———— * ————

ANNIBALE CARRACCI, *FLIGHT INTO EGYPT*, c.1604

# NOTES

1   Fehl P P, *The classical monument; reflections on the connection between morality and art in Greek and Roman sculpture*, New York 1972.

2   eg Shetelig, H, *Classical impulses in Scandinavian art from the migration period to the Viking age*, Oslo 1949 (Instituttet for sammenlignende kulturforskning. Serie A: Forelesninger, 19; Romanini, A M, 1976 'Il concetto di classico e l'arte medievale', *Romano Barbarica* 1, 203-42.

3   Allen, T, *A classical revival in Islamic architecture*, Wiesbaden 1986; Powers, M J, 'The dialectic of classicism in early Imperial China' *Art Journal* 47.1-88, 20-5.

4   Powers 1988, 22, 24-5. For a diverging view see Hay, 'Some questions concerning classicism in relation to Chinese painting', *Art Journal* 47.1-88, 26-34;

5   Hersey, G, *The lost meaning of classical architecture. Speculations on ornament from Vitruvius to Venturi*, Cambridge MA & London 1988, 1.

6   Greenhalgh, M, *Donatello and his Sources*. London 1982; Spencer, J R, 'Speculations on the origins of the Italian Renaissance medal', *Studies in the History of Art* (NG Washington) 21, 1987, 197-203; he suggests medallists may have known and used pottery lamps and even Etruscan mirrors; Vermeule, C C, 'Graeco-Roman Asia Minor to Renaissance Italy: medallic and related arts', *ibid*, 263-81, suggests (264) that 'the Greek coins of Asia Minor under the Romans played an important, heretofor-undocumented part in the classical awakening from the early 1400s to the late 1500s'; and he makes some very attracive comparanda with B di Giovanni, Boldu, and Pisanello, as well as Matteo de'Pasti.

7   Krier, L, 'An architecture of desire' *Architectural Design* 56, 4, 1986, note 3.

8   eg Toggenburger, K, *Die Werkstatt der deutschen Klassik: Goethes und Schillers Diskussion des kunstlerischen Shaffens*, (Zurcher Beiträge zür deutschen Literatur und Geistesgeschichte), Zurich 1948; and Weisinger, K D, *The classical façade: a nonclassical reading of Goethe's classicism*, University Park, PA, 1988.

9   eg Boulter, C G, ed, *Greek art, archaic into classical* (symposium, University of Cincinnati, 1982), Leiden 1985.

10   eg Hardtwig, B, ed, Catalogue of the Neue Pinakothek, Munich: *Nach-Barock und Klassizismus*, Munich 1978.

11   Wallace, R K, *Jane Austen and Mozart: classical equilibrium in fiction and music*, Athens, Georgia, 1983; see Kermode, F, *The Classic*, London 1975, for a brief definition of classicism in literature.

12   Zerner, H, 'Classicism as power', *Art Journal* 47.1-88, 35-6. See 36: 'The art of Caravaggio had been despised as crude unartistic realism. In the process of being made the equal of classicism, his baroque style has in fact become a type of classicism.'

13   Rodenwalt, G, 'Zür begrifflichen und geschichtlichen Bedeutung des Klassizismus in der Bildenden Kunst. Eine kunstphilosophische Studie', *Zeitschrift fuer Aesth. und allg. Kunstwiss.* 11, 1916, 113-31; Wall, K A, *A classical philosophy of art: the nature of art in the light of classical principles*, Washington DC 1982.

14   Greenhalgh, M, *The classical tradition in art*, London 1978.

15   Highet, G, *The classical tradition. Greek and Roman influences on western literature*, Oxford 1949.

16   Saxl, F, 'The classical inscription in Renaissance art and politics', *Journal of the Warburg & Courtauld Institutes* (hereafter *JWCI*) 4, 1941, 19-46; Morison, S, *Politics and script. Aspects of authority and freedom in the development of Graeco-Latin script*, Oxford 1972; Calabi Limentani, I, 'Sul non saper leggere le epigrafi classiche nei secoli 12 e 13; sulla scoperta graduale delle abbreviazioni epigrafiche', *Acme* 23, 1970, 253-82. And cf Poggio Bracciolini's use of his epigraphical knowledge in his funeral orations: Kajanto, I, 'Poggio Bracciolini

and classical epigraphy', *Arctos (Acta Philologica Fennica)* XIX, 1985, 19-40.

17 Klawans, Z H, *Imitations and inventions of Roman coins. Renaissance medals of Julius Caesar and the Roman Empire,* Santa Monica 1977, and a series of articles by Wentzel, H: 'Der Augustalis Friedrichs II und die abendlandische Glyptik des 13. Jahrhunderts', *Zeitschrift fuer Kunstgeschichte* (hereafter *ZfKG*) 15, 1952, 183-7; 'Portraits "à l'antique" on French medieval gems and seals', *JWCI* 16, 1953, 342-50; 'Italienische Siegelstempel und Siegel all'antico im 13. und 14. Jahrhundert' *Mitteilungen Kunsthistorisches Instituts in Florenz}*17, 1955, 73-86; 'Antiken-imitationen des 12. und 13. Jahrhunderts in Italien" *ZfKW* 9, 1955, 29-72; and 'Staatskameen' im Mittelalter', *JBuch Berl Museen* 4, 1962, 42-77.

18 Max Radin in *The Encyclopaedia of the Social Sciences,* New York 1959, XV, 63, sv *tradition.*

19 Buck, A, & Pfister, M, *Studien zu den 'Volgarizzamenti' roemischer Autoren in der italienischen Literatur des 13 und 14 Jahrhunderts,* Munich 1978.

20 Adhemar, J, *Influences antiques dans l'art du moyen âge français; recherches sur les sources et les thèmes d'inspiration,* London 1939; Bracco, V, *L'archeologia classica nella cultura occidentale,* Rome 1979; Chiri, G, 'La cultura classica nella coscienza medioevale', *Studi Romani* 2, 1954, 395-410. *The Oxford Art Journal* 3.2, 1980 is devoted to the theme of propaganda.

21 Lord, G de F, *Classical presences in 17th-century English poetry,* New Haven 1987.

22 Kristeller, P O, *Renaissance thought: the classic, scholastic, and humanistic strains,* rev ed, New York 1961.

23 Drexler, A, editor, *The architecture of the Ecole des Beaux-Arts,* London 1977; see Chafee, R, 'The teaching of architecture at the Ecole des Beaux-Arts', 61-109, especially 63.

24 Pevsner, N, *Academies of art, past and present,* Cambridge 1940; see the Italian edition of Antonio Pinelli, *Le accademie d'arte,* Turin 1982, updated bibliography pp. xliii-xlviii; Barocchi, P, *L'Accademia Etrusca* (exhibition, Cortona, Palazzo Casali), Milan 1985; or Harari, M, 'Toscanita = Etruschita. Da modello a mito storiografico: le origini settecentesche', *Xenia* 15, 1988, 65-72, with plentiful bibliography; Hughes, A, 'An academy for doing: II: academies, status and power in early modern Europe', *Oxford Art Jnl* 9.2, 1986, 50-62, with useful bibliographical note at 61-2 which updates Pevsner & Schlosser-Magnino; Viala, A, *Naissance de l'écrivain: sociologie de la litterature à l'âge classique,* Paris 1985; see ch I, on the rise of the academies.

25 Carlsen, H, *A bibliography to the classical tradition in English literature,* Copenhagen 1985; Smith, E, *A dictionary of classical reference in English poetry,* Woodbridge, Suffolk, & Totowa, NJ 1984; Pechter, E, *Dryden's classical theory of literature,* London etc. 1975; Gallaway, F, *Reason, rule, and revolt in English classicism,* New York 1965; Kallendorf, C, *Latin influences on English literature from the Middle Ages to the 18th Century: an annotated bibliography of scholarship,* 1945-1979, New York 1982.

26 eg Bolgar, R R, editor, *Classical influences on Western thought, A.D. 1650-1870,* Cambridge 1979.

27 Pochat, G, *Geschichte der Aesthetik und Kunsttheorie von der Antike bis zum 19 Jahrhundert,* Cologne 1986, with excellent bibliography.

28 Toubert, 'Rome et le Mont-Cassin', *Dumbarton Oaks Papers* 30, 1976, 3-33.

29 Cochrane, CN, *Christianity and classical culture,* Oxford 1940; Seznec, J, *The survival of the pagan gods,* New York 1953; Panofsky, E & Saxl, F, 'Classical mythology in medieval art', *Metropolitan Museum Studies* 4, 1933, 228-80; Saxl, F, 'Pagan and Jewish elements in Early Christian sculpture', in his *Lectures,* London 1957, 45-57; Weitzmann, K, 'The survival of mythological representations in Early Christian and Byzantine art and their impact on Christian iconography', *DOP* 14, 1960, 45-68; Hamann-Maclean, RHL, 'Antikenstudium in der Kunst des Mittelalters', *Marburger JBuch* 15, 1949-50, 157-250; Swift, EH, *Roman sources of Christian art* New York 1951; Schweitzer, B, *Die spaetantiken Grundlagen der mittelalterlichen Kunst,* Leipzig 1949; Taylor, HO, *The classical heritage of the middle ages,* rev ed New York 1957;

30 Oakeshott, WF, *Classical inspiration in medieval art,* London 1959.

31 Lindgren, C, *Classical art forms and Celtic mutations: figural art in Roman Britain,* Park Ridge, NJ, 1980.

32 Pavan, M, *Antichità classica e pensiero moderno,* Florence 1977, 345-59: 'Classicità e classicismo nel guidizio sul mondo antico'; Niemeier, J-P., *Kopien und Nachahmungen im Hellenismus: ein Beitrag zum Klassizismus des 2. und fruhen 1. Jahrhunderts vor Chr,* Bonn 1985.

33 Lallanzi, A D, *'Linea di Apelle' e altre eredita trasmesse dalla tecnica pittorica ellenistica all' arte bizantina e occidentale medievale: osservazioni ed ipotesi* (Accad. Scienze Lettere ed Arti di Palermo, Classe di Scienze Morali e Filologiche, Memorie I), Palermo 1979; Weitzmann, K, *The Classical heritage in Byzantine and Near Eastern art,* London 1981.

34 Adhémar, J, *Influences antiques dans l'art du moyen âge français; recherches sur les sources et les thèmes d'inspiration,* London 1939; Bracco, V, *L'archeologia classica nella cultura occidentale,* Romek 1979; Chiri, G, 'La cultura classica nella coscienza medioevale', *Studi Romani* 2, 1954, 395-410.

35 Deichmann, F W, 'Die Spolien in der spaetantiken Architektur', in *Bayerische Akademie der Wissenschaften, Phil.-Hist. Klasse: Sitzungsberichte,* 1975, Heft 6; Deichmann, F W, 'Il materiale di spoglio nell'architettura tardoantica', *Corsi di Cultura sull'arte ravennate e bizantina* 23, 1976, 131-46; Esch, A, 'Spolien. Zur Wiederverwendung antiker Baustucke und Skulpturen im mittelalterlichen Italien', *Archiv fuer Kulturgeschichte* 51, 1969, 1-64.

35 Caldwell, M P, *The public display of antique sculpture in Venice, 1200-1600,* PhD thesis, London University, 1975.

36 *Charlemagne: oeuvre, rayonnement et survivances,* Council of Europe Exhibition, Aix la Chapelle, 1965; Braunfels, W, 'Karls des Grossen Bronzewerkstatt' in W. Braunfels (editor), *Karl der Grosse: Lebenswerk und Nachleben, 3: Karolingische Kunst,* Dusseldorf 1965, 168-202; Fillitz, H, 'L'arte alla corte di Carlo Magno nei suoi rapporti con l'antichità. A proposito del problema della scultura in avorio carolingia', *Rendiconti Pont. Accad. Romana d'Archeologia* 38, 1965, 221-36; McClendon, C B, 'The revival of opus sectile pavements in Rome and the vicinity in the Carolingian period', *Papers of the British School at Rome* 48, 1980, 157-65; D'Onofrio, M, *Roma e Aquisgrana,* Rome 1983.

37 Cowdrey, HEJ, *The age of Abbot Desiderius. Montecassino, the Papacy and the Normans in the 11th and early 12th century,* Oxford 1983; Deer, J, *The dynastic porphyry tombs of the Norman period in Sicily* (Dumbarton Oaks Studies 5), Cambridge, Mass. 1959; Carbonara, G, *Iussu Desiderii: Montecassino e l'architettura campano-abruzzese nell'undicesimo secolo,* Rome 1979.

38 Conference: *Federico II e l'arte del Duecento Italiano* (Atti 3 Cong. Sett. Studi di Storia dell'Arte dell'Universita di Roma, 1978), 2 vols, Lecce 1980; Giuliano, A, 'Motivi classici nella scultura e nella critica di età normanna e federiciana', in *ibid.* 1, 19-26; Claussen, P C, 'Scultura romana al tempo di Federico II', in *ibid.* 1, 325-8.

39 Demus, O, 'A renascence of Early Christian art in the 13th century in Venice', in Weitzmann, K (ed), *Late classical and medieval studies in honour of AM Friend Jnr,* Princeton 1955, 348-61; Gandolfo, F, 'Reimpiego di sculture antiche nei troni papali del 12 secolo', *Att. Pont. Acca. Rom. Arch.: Rendiconti* 47, 1974-5, 203--8; Heckscher, W S, *Aeneas insignes statuas romano populo restituendas censuit,* The Hague, n.d.; Rodocanachi, E, 'Les anciens monuments de Rome du 15e au 18e siècle: attitude du Saint Siège et du Conseil communal à leur égard', *Revue Archéologique* 4, 1913, 171-83; Telpaz, A M, 'Some antique motifs in Trecento art', *AB* 46, 1964, 372-6; Pacht, O, 'The precarolingian roots of early romanesque art', *Acts 20th Int. Cong. History of Art* 1, Princeton 1963, 67-75. See also several of the classic papers by Krautheimer, R, all now reprinted, with revisions and updates, in his *Studies in Early Christian, Medieval and Renaissance art,* London 1971, especially his 'Introduction to an iconography of medieval architecture', 115-50, and 'The Carolingian revival of Early Christian architecture', 203-56.

40 Kitzinger, E, 'The Hellenistic heritage in Byzantine art reconsidered' in *16 Internationaler Byzantinistenkongress, Vienna 1981, Akten 1/2,* (Jahrbuch der

ost.' Byzantinistik 31/1-2-3), Vienna 1982, 657-75; Van der Vin, J P A, *Travellers to Greece and Constantinople. Ancient monuments and old traditions in medieval travellers' tales*, (Uitgaven van het Nederlands Historisch-Archaeologisch Instituut te Istanbul, 49), 2 vols, Leiden 1980.

41 Rosenthal, E, 'Classical elements in Carolingian illustration', *La Bibliofilia* 55, 1953, 85-106; Schwartz, J, 'Quelques sources antiques d'ivoires carolingiens', *Cahiers Archéologiques* 11, 1960, 145-62. That classical ideas and motifs do not need an overtly classical style is evident from, for example, the Trés Riches Heures: cf. Bath, M, 'Imperial renovation symbolism in the Trés Riches Heures', *Simiolus* 17.1, 1987, 5-22.

42 Deschamps, P, 'Etude sur la renaissance de la sculpture à l'époque romane', *Bull. Monumental* 84, 1925, 5-98; Keller, H, *Das Nachleben des antiken Bildnisses von der Karolingerzeit bis zür Gegenwart*, Freiburg etc. 1970; Von Einem, H, 'Die Monumental Plastik des Mittelalters und ihr Verhaeltnis zür Antike', *Antike und Abendland* 3, 1948, 120-51; Sauerlaender, W, 'Art antique et sculpture autour 1200', *Art de France* 1, 1961, 47-56.

43 Graf, A, *Roma nella memoria e nelle immaginazioni del medio evo*, Turin 1915; Dacos, N, *La découverte de la Domus Aurea et la formation des grotesques à la Renaissance*, London/Leiden 1969; Heckscher, W S, *Die Romruinen. Die geistige Voraussetzungen ihrer Wertung im Mittelalter und in der Renaissance*, Dissertation, Hamburg 1936; for a later period, Pietrangeli, G, The discovery of classical sculpture in 18th-century Rome', *Apollo* 117, May 1983, 380-91.

44 Smith, E B, *Architectural symbolism of Imperial Rome and the Middle Ages*, Princeton 1956.

45 Fevrier, P A, 'Permanence et héritages de l'antiquite dans la topographie des villes de l'Occident durant le haut moyen âge', in *Topografia urbana e vita cittadina nell'Alto Medioevo in Occidente* (Sett. di Studio del CISAM 21, Spoleto 1973), Spoleto 1974, 41-138; Greenhalgh, M, 'Ipsa ruina docet: l'uso del antico nel Medioevo', in S. Settis editor, *Memoria dell'antico ne ll'arte italiana, 1: L'uso dei classici*, Turin 1984, 115-167; Greenhalgh, M, *The survival of Roman antiquities in medieval Europe*, London 1989.

46 Arenhoevel, W, editor, *Berlin und die Antike*, Exhibition, Staatliche Museen, Preussischer Kulturbesitz, 2 vols, Berlin 1979.

47 Ladendorf, H, *Antikenstudium und Antikenkopie: Vorarbeitung zu einer Darstellung ihrer Bedeutung in der mittelalterlichen und neueren Zeit*, rev ed, Berlin 1958; *La cultura antica nell'Occidente latino dal 7 al 11 secolo* (Conference: 22 Sett. di Studio del CISAM, 1974), 2 vols Spoleto 1975.

48 Micheli, M E, 'Le raccolte di antichità di Antonio Canova', *Rivista dell'Istituto Nazionale di Archeologia e Storia dell'Arte* VIII-IX, 1985-6, 205-322. Canova had some splendid Italic terracottas from temple revetments: is he the first artist known to have collected these – or should we imagine people like Ghiberti and Donatello collecting similar material?

49 Panofsky, E, *Renaissance and renascences in Western art*, Stockholm 1960; Wessel, K, 'Antikenrezeption in der Kunst, 2: Byzanz', *Lexikon des Mittelalters* 1.4, 1979, 714f.; Weitzmann, K, editor, *The age of spirituality: a symposium*, New York 1980; Beck, H G, 'Constantinople; the rise of a new capital in the East', in *ibid*, 29-37.

50 For a general survey, see Thomas, T M, *Classical reliefs and statues in later Quattrocento religious paintings*, Ph.D., Berkeley CA 1980.

51 Hearn, M F, *Romanesque sculpture. The revival of monumental stone sculpture in the 11th and 12th centuries*, Oxford 1981.

52 De Jong, J L, De Oudheid in *Fresco. De interpretatie van klassieke onderwerpen in de Italiaanse wandschilderkunst, inzonderheid te Rome, circa 1370-1555*, PhD, Leiden 1987, with English summary.

53 Beck H, & Blum, D, editors, *Natur und Antike in der Renaissance*, (Exhibition, Liebighaus, Museum alter Plasti, 1985-6), Frankfurt-am-Main 1985.

54 eg Seidel, M, 'Studien zur Antikenrezeption Nicola Pisanos', *Mitt KHIF* 19, 1975, 307-92; and, generally, Vermeule, C C, *European art and the classical past*, Cambridge Mass, 1964.

55 eg Amory, D, 'Masaccio's *Expulsion from Paradise:* a recollection of antiq-

uity', *Marsyas* XX, 1979-80, 7-10; Tresidder, W D, *The classicism of the early works of Titian: its sources and character* (PhD dissertation, University of Michigan), Ann Arbor 1979.

56 Becatti, G, 'Raphael and antiquity', in Salmi, M, editor, *The complete work of Raphael*, Novara 1969, 491-568; and Castagnoli, F, 'Raphael and ancient Rome', in *ibid*, 569-84.

57 For a full discussion of Raphael, see Greenhalgh 1978, 93-110.

58 Fraser, V, 'Architecture and imperialism in 16th-century Spanish America', *Art History* 9, 1986, 325-35: see 332.

59 Drew, P, *Third generation: the changing meaning of architecture*, London 1972, 39.

60 Tzonis A, & Lefaivre, L, *Classical architecture: the poetics of order*, Cambridge, Mass 1986: *investigates the poetics of classical architecture* (ix); Smith, T G *Classical architecture: rule and invention*, Layton, Utah 1988.

61 Bruschi, A, *Bramante*, Eng. trans. London 1977, 87-113: 'Bramante's *grand manner*: the Belvedere and the revival of the classical villa.'

62 Wiebenson, D, editor, *Architectural theory and practice from Alberti to Ledoux*, Chicago 1982.

63 Lehmann, P W, 'Alberti and antiquity: additional observations' *Art Bulletin* LXX.3, 1988, 388-400.

64 Fancelli, M, *Palladio e Praeneste*, Rome 1974.

65 Forssman E *et al, Palladio, la sua eredita nel mondo*, Milan 1980; Farber J C, & Reed, H H, *Palladio's architecture and its influence: a photographic guide*, New York 1980 (on the UK & USA); Harris, J, *The Palladians*, London 1981; Guinness B, & Sadler, J T, *The Palladian style in England, Ireland and America*, London 1976; Wittkower, R, *Palladio and English Palladianism*, London 1974.

66 Millar, J F, *Classical architecture in Renaissance Europe 1419-1585*, Williamsburg, VA 1987.

67 Archer, J, 'Rus in urbe: classical ideals of country and city in British town planning', *Studies in 18th-C. Culture* XII, ed. H C Payne, Madison WI 1983.

68 Beck J, & Bol, P C, editors, *Forschungen zur Villa Albani: antike Kunst und die Epoche der Aufklarung*, Berlin 1982 (Frankfurter Forschungen zur Kunst, Bd. 10). See also Capecchi, G *et al*, editors, La *Villa di Poggio Reale*, Rome 1979, for a Florentine version of the same, largely 17th and 19th centuries.

69 Pasquali, M, editor, *Pompei e il recupero del classico*, exhibition, Ancona, Palazzo Bosdari, 1980, for the background.

70 Cust, L *History of the Society of Dilettanti*, London 1914.

71 Duncan, C, & Wallach, A, 'The universal survey museum', *Art History* 3.4, 1980, 448-69, especially 448ff: 'Museums as ceremonial architecture'.

72 Beck, H, editor, *Antikensammlungen im 18. Jahrhundert*, Berlin 1981 (Frankfurter Forschungen zur Kunst, Bd. 9): 129-48 for Mengs; 11928 for the Villa Albani; 295ff. for English collections. The best summary of British collecting is still Michaelis, A, *Ancient marbles in Great Britain*, Cambridge 1882, 1-184.

73 Crimp, 'The end of art and the origin of the museum' *Art Journal* 46.-87, 261-6.

74 Cited by Haskell, F, 'The artist and the museum', *The New York Review of Books*, XXXIV.19, 1987, 38-42: see 42.

75 Wyss, B, 'Klassizismus und Kulturpolitik im Konflikt. Aloys Hirt und Hegel' in Poeggeler O, & Gethmann-Siefert, A-M, editors, *Kunstfahrung und Kulturpolitik im Berlin Hegels* (Hegel Studien Supp. 22), Bonn 1983.

76 Crimp 1987, 264, from the A*esthetics;* cited from Paolucci, H, editor, *Hegel on the Arts*, New York 1979, 37-8.

77 Momigliano, A, 'Ancient history and the antiquarian', *JWCI* XIII, 1950, 285-315; Bergdoll, B, 'Archaeology vs. history: Heinrich Huebsch's critique of neoclassicism and the beginnings of historicism in German architectural theory', *Oxford Art Jnl* 5.2 1983, 3-12; Rykwert, J, *The first moderns: the architects of the 18th century*, Cambridge Mass 1980, explains the shift from the classical to the neoclassic mode.

78 Bracken, C P, *Antiquities acquired: the spoliation of Greece*, Newton Abbot 1975.

79  Cust 1914, 38f.

80  For a discussion of how artistic and social change are related, cf Boime, A, *Art in an age of Revolution, 1750-1800* (A social history of modern art, I), Chicago & London 1987; Eitner, L, *Neoclassicism and romanticism: 1750-1850. Sources and documents*, Englewood Cliffs NJ 1971; and Hadjinicolaou, N, *La lutte des classes en France dans la production d'images de 1829 à 1831. Première partie: la critique d'art*, Thèse d'Etat, Ecole des Hautes Etudes en Sciences Sociales, Paris 1980. See the excerpt from this, 'Art in a period of social upheaval', in *Oxford Art Journal* 6.2, 1983, 29-37.

81  Haskell, F, *Rediscoveries in art. Some aspects of taste, fashion and collecting in England and France*, London 1976.

82  Rump, G C, editor, *Kunst und Kunsttheorie des XVIII Jahrhunderts in England: Studien zum Wandel aesthetische Anschauungen, 1650-1830*, Hildesheim 1979; Weinbrot, H D, *Augustus Caesar in 'Augustan' England: the decline of a classical norm*, Princeton, NJ 1978; Warmer E, & Hough G, *Strangeness and beauty: an anthology of aesthetic criticism 1840-1910, I: Ruskin to Swinburne*, Cambridge etc. 1983.

83  Stainton, L, editor, *British artists in Rome, 1700-1800* (exhibition, Kenwood House), London 1974; Hope, A M, *The theory and practice of Neoclassicism in English painting: the origins, development and decline of an ideal*, New York 1988; Keisch, C, editor, *Classici e romantici tedeschi in Italia: opere d'arte dei musei della Repubblica democratica tedesca* (exhibition, Venice), Venice 1977; Gerlach, P, *Antikenstudien in Zeichnungen klassisistischer Bildhauer*, Munich 1973.

84  Wood, C, *Olympian dreamers: Victorian classical painters, 1860-1914*, London 1983.

85  Kestner, J A, *Mythology and misogyny. The social discourse of 19th-century British classical-subject painting*, Madison, Wisconsin & London, 1989.

86  Smith, A D, 'The *historical revival* in late 18th-century England and France', *Art History* 2.2, 1979, 156-78. This is a quantitative survey, with tables, which concludes that in England 'the return to classical antiquity, so loudly trumpeted, was largely still born' (169).

87  Benot, Y, editor, *Le Pour et le Contre. Correspondence polémique sur le respect de la postérité*, Paris 1958; see also Seznec, J, *Essais sur Diderot et l'Antiquite*, Oxford 1957.

88  Which, it has been suggested, Gibbon resolved by the conflation of antique ideas and modern scholarship: Levine, J M, 'Ancients and moderns reconsidered', *18th-Century Studies* 15, 1981-2, 72-89.

89  Hamilton, G H, *Painting & Sculpture in Europe, 1880-1940*, Harmondsworth 1967, 5.

90  *In her literature, art, thought and general culture we find nothing of value which is not a dull echo of Greece:* Bell, C, *Civilisation*, West Drayton 1938, 32.

91  Rosenblum, R, *The international style of 1800: a study in linear abstraction*, New York 1976; Symmons, S, *Flaxman and Europe: the outline illustrations and their influence*, New York 1984; Hofmann, W, editor, *John Flaxman: Mythologie und Industrie: Kunst um 1800* (exhibition, Hamburger Kunsthalle, 1979), Munich 1979.

92  Bell, op cit, 53, 128ff: for Bell, work seems inimical to culture.

93  *Ein griechische Traum. Leo von Klenze der Archaeologe*, (exhibition, Glyptothek), Munich 1985.

94  Cf his work on polychromy in the ancient world: von Buttlar, A, 'Klenzes Beitrag zür Polychromie-Frage, *Ein griechisches Traum*, Munich 1985, 213-23.

95  Kelder, D, *Aspects of 'official' painting and philosophic art, 1789-1799*, New York 1976; Paulson, R, *Representations of revolution (1789-1820)*, New Haven 1983; *French painting 1774-1830, the Age of Revolution* (exhibition, Paris, Detroit & New York 1974-5), Detroit 1975; Parker, H T, *The cult of antiquity and the French revolutionaries: a study in the development of the revolutionary spirit*, Chicago 1937; Sturmer, M, *Scherben des Glucks: Klassizismus und Revolution*, Berlin 1987; Briganti, G, *I pittori dell' immaginario: arte e rivoluzione psicologica*, Milan 1977.

96  Mainardi, P, *Art and politics of the Second Empire: the Universal Expositions of 1855 and 1867*, New Haven 1987.

97  Boime, A, 'Declassicising the academic: a realist view of Ingres', *Art History* 8.1, 1985, 50-65.

98  Wattenmaker, R J, *Puvis de Chavannes and the modern tradition* (exhibition, Art Gallery of Ontario), Toronto 1975.

99  Brendel, O J, 'Classic and non-classic elements in Picasso's *Guernica'*, in Oates, W J, ed, *From Sophocles to Picasso: the present-day vitality of the classical tradition*, Bloomington IN, 1962, 121-59; also his 'The classical style in modern art', *ibid*, 71-118, especially 124; Haskell F, & Penny, N, *Taste and the antique: the lure of classical sculpture, 1500-1900*, New Haven and London 1981: see the epilogue, 117-24.

100  Haskell and Penny 1981, 79-91: 'The proliferation of casts and copies'.

101  Honour, H, 'Neoclassicism' in *The age of Neo-Classicism* (exhibition, Royal Academy), London 1972, xxi-xxix, for a short discussion. True Neoclassicism has an intimate relationship with invigorating discoveries: see Raspi Serra J, and Simoncini, G, eds, *La fortuna di Paestum e la memoria moderna del dorico 1750-1830*, (exhibition, Salerno 1986), 2 vols, Florence 1986.

102  Tuerr, K, *Zur Antikenrezeption in der franzoesischen Skulptur des 19 und fruehen 20. Jahrhunderts*, Berlin 1979.

103  Hartmann, J B, *Antike Motive bei Thorvaldsen: Studien zur Antikenrezeption des Klassizismus*, Tubingen 1979, with a comparison between the sources and their interpretation.

104  Mumford, L, 'The basis of universalism', in his *Roots of contemporary American architecture*, 2nd ed, New York 1959, 369-81: see 370.

105  Alsop, J, *The rare art traditions. The history of art collecting and its linked phenomena wherever these have appeared*, London 1982; Haskell, F, ed, *Saloni gallerie, musei e loro influenza sullo sviluppo dell' arte dei secoli XIX e XX*, being vol VII of the *XXIV Congresso Internazionale della Storia dell'Arte*, Bologna 1982.

106  Kuhn, B, 'Francesco Pascucci – ein Beitrag zum roemischen Klassizismus', *Roem. Hist. Mitt. Oest. Akad. Wiss., Historisches Institut, Rom) , 28*, 1986, 387-425, for a well-referenced guide to this terminology.

107  Pach, W, *The classical tradition in modern art*, London 1959, 20-28.

108  Pach 1959, 56.

109  eg Firedel, H, editor, *Der Traum des Orpheus: Mythologie in der italienischen Gegenwartskunst 1967 bis 1984* (exhibition, Staedische Galerie im Lenbachhaus), Munich 1984; Whiteley, J J L, *The revival in painting of themes inspired by Antiquity in mid-19th-century France*, D.Phil thesis, Oxford 1972.

110  Traeger, J, *Der Weg nach Valhalla. Denkmallandschaft und Bildungsreise im 19. Jahrhundert*, Regesnburg 1987, with a copious bibliography.

111  eg Lundwall, S, *Generationsvaxlingen inom romantikens Klassicism*, Stockholm 1960 (Nordiska Museets handlingar, 54) for Swedish material.

112  Wilton-Ely, J, *The mind and art of Giovanni Battista Piranesi*, London 1978.

113  Canat, R, *La renaissance de la Grèce antique, 1820-50*, Paris 1911; Treves, P, editor, *Lo studio dell'antichita classica nell'Ottocento*, 5 vols in 6, Milan & Naples 1962. The terminological confusion is very clear from the title of Bertrand, L, *La fin du classicisme et le retour à l'antique . . . en France*, Paris 1896; Pavan M, *Antichita classica e pensiero moderno*, Florence 1977, 159-210: 'Gli *Elgin Marbles* e il recupero dell'Ellenico'; see also Barzun, J, *Classic, romantic and modern*, rev ed, London 1962.

114  Lalumia, M P, *Realism and politics in Victorian art of the Crimean War*, Ann Arbor 1984, for the abandonment of 'the heroising mode'; and Hofmann, W, *et al, Shrecken und Hoffnung. Kuenstler sehen Frieden und Krieg* (exhibition, Hamburg, Moscow etc 1987-8), for changing attitudes to the depiction of war.

115  Shankman, S, *Pope's Iliad: Homer in the age of passion*, Princeton, NJ 1983.

116  Rubel, M M, *Savage and barbarian: historical attitudes in the criticism of Homer and Ossian in Britain, 1760-1800*, Amsterdam 1978.

117  Goldstein, C, 'Toward a definition of academic art' *Art Bulletin* LVII, 1975, 102-9; Hess, T B, and Asbery, J, editors, 'The Academy. Five centuries of

grandeur and misery from the Carracci to Mao Tse-Tung', *Art News Annual* XXXIII, 1967.

118 Hutchison, SC, *The history of the Royal Academy, 1768-1968*, London 1968; Morgan, HC, 'The lost opportunity of the Royal Academy', *Jnl. Warburg and Courtauld Institutes* XXXII, 1969, 410-20, charts its decline; and now see *Apollo* CXXVIII, Oct 1988, the theme of which is *The Royal Academy* revisited.

119 Boime, A, *The Academy and French painting in the 19th century*, London 1971.

120 Salerno, L, 'Immobilismo politico e accademica', *in Storia dell' arte Einaudi*, VI.1, Turin 1981, 449-522; Pinto S, *et al*, editors, *Cultura classica e romantica nella Toscana granducale. Sfortuna dell' Accademia*, exhibition catalogue, Florence 1972; Caramel, L, and Poli, F, *L'arte bella. La questione delle Accademie di belle arti*, Milan 1979.

121 Bordieu, P, 'The academic eye: from nomos to the institutionalisation of anomie', *Art and Text* 28 1988, 4-19: see 5.

122 Iversen, M, 'Politics and the historiography of art history: Woelfflin's Classic Art', *Oxford Art Journal* 4.1, 1981, 31-4.

123 cf Paet, P, T*he Berlin Secession: modernism and its enemies in imperial Germany*, Cambridge, Mass. 1980. See 1: *although few of its artists were actually political, the antagonism felt toward the avant-garde by those who dispensed state patronage . . . turned the founding of the secession itself into a political act.*

124 Max Radin again, in *The Encyclopaedia of the Social Sciences, loc cit: a tradition is not a mere observed fact, like an existing custom . . . ; it is an idea which expresses a value judgment. A certain way of acting is regarded as right; a certain order or arrangement is held desirable. The maintenance of the tradition is the assertion of this judgment.*

125 Meyer Shapiro in *The Encyclopaedia of the Social Sciences* New York 1959, XIV, 524, sv *taste.*

126 In 1935: Chipp, HB, *Theories of modern art*, Berkeley and London 1968, 271.

127 *Futurist Painting: Technical Manifesto*, of 1910; from Chipp 1968, 289.

128 Gleizes A, and Metzinger, J, *Du Cubisme*, Eng. trans London 1913; quoted from Chipp 1968, 207.

129 quoted from Chipp 1968, 298-9.

130 *ibid*, 301.

131 Janson, H W, editor, *La scultura del XIX secolo, passim* (being vol 6 of the *Atti del XXIV Congresso Internazionale della Storia dell' Arte*, Bologna 1982); see especially, Benge, G F, 'Barye, Flaxman and Phidias', 103-110.

132 Elsen, A E, *Origins of modern sculpture: pioneers and premises* rev ed, London 1974, 155.

133 Wiebenson, D, *Sources of Greek revival architecture*, University Park, Penn 1969, for a list of the publications involved.

134 Raspi Serra 1986.

135 Crook, J M *The Greek revival: Neo-Classical attitudes in British architecture, 1760-1870*, London 1972; Rykwert, J, *The first moderns: the architects of the 18th century*, Cambridge, Mass 1980; Rykwert, J, 'Order in building' *Res* 11, Spring 1986, 5-16; *ibid*, 'On the oral transmission of architectural theory', *Res* 3, Spring 1982, 68-81; Vidler, A, *The writing of the walls: architectural theory in the late enlightenment*, Princeton, NJ, 1987.

136 Alexander, D B, *The sources of classicism: five centuries of architectural books from the collections of the Humanities Research Center*, Austin 1978.

137 Archer, J, *The literature of domestic architecture 1715-1842*, Cambridge MT & London 1985, 34-9 with notes and copious examples (eg George Richardson, entry 283.2).

138 Reudenbach, B, *G. B. Piranesi, Architektur als Bild: der Wandel in der Architekturauffassung des achtzehnten Jahrhunderts*, Munich 1979.

139 Rosenau, H, *Boullée & visionary architecture* London 1976.

140 Du Prey, P de la R, *John Soane, the making of an architect*, Chicago 1982; Dunster, D, editor, *John Soane*, Architectural Monographs series, London 1983: see Watkin, D, 'Soane and his contemporaries', 40-59.

141 Collins, P, *Changing ideals in modern architecture, 1750-1950*, London 1965, 198-217.

142 Beard, G W, *The work of Robert Adam*, Edinburgh 1978.

143 eg Watkin, D, *The triumph of the classical: Cambridge architecture, 1804-1834*, (exhibition, Fitzwilliam Museum), Cambridge 1977.

144 Levine, N, 'The Romantic idea of architectural legibility: Henri Labrouste and the Neo-Grec', in Drexler 1977, 325-416: quote from 329. For an example of the relationship between archaeology and 19th-century architecture, see Hederer, O, *Leo von Klenze: Persoenlichkeit und Werke*, Munich, rev ed.1981. 184ff for his Glyptothek at Munich.

145 *Berlin und die Antike: Architektur, Kunstgewerbe, Malerei, Skulptur, Theater und Wissenschaft vom 16. Jahrhundert bis heute* (Exhibition, Berlin, Schloss Charlottenburg, Grosse Orangerie, 1979), Berlin 1979; Bloch, P *Das klassische Berlin: d. Berliner Bildhauerschule im 19. Jahrhunderts*, Frankfurt am Main etc. 1978; Schinkel, K F, *Collected architectural designs*, London 1982.

146 Nikolaev, E V, *Klassicheskaia Moskva*, Moscow 1975.

147 Pevsner, N, *A history of building types*, London 1976, 293.

148 Crook, J M, *The dilemma of style: architectural ideas from the Picturesque to the Post-Modern*, Chicago 1988.

149 K Dohmer, *In welchem Style sollen wir bauen?: Architekturtheorie zwischen Klassizismus u. Jugendstil*, Munich 1976 (Studien zur Kunst des neunzehnten Jahrhunderts, Bd. 36): the title comes from the architect Heinrich Huebsch's pamphlet of 1828).

150 Braham, A, *The architecture of the French Enlightenment* Berkeley 1980; Middleton, R, & Watkin, D, *Neoclassical and 19th-century architecture*, New York 1980; *Soufflot et son temps: 1780-1980*, (Exhibition, Paris, Caisse Nationale des Monuments Historiques et des Sites, 1980-1), Paris 1980.

151 Collins 1965, 61-146.

152 Egbert, D D, *The Beaux-Arts tradition in French architecture*, Princeton 1980, 5ff., 42ff.

153 Illustrated in *Architectural Design* 56, 4, 1986, 39-40.

154 Allwood, J, *The great exhibitions*, London 1977; Greenhalgh, P, *Ephemeral vistas: the expositions universelles, great exhibitions and world's fairs, 1851-1939*, Manchester 1988, with excellent bibliography.

155 Daniel Burnham, Director of Works for the Columbian Exposition in Chicago, 1893. Cited from Fitch, J M, *American building, I: the historical forces that shaped it*, Boston & Cambridge MA 1966, 212.

156 Sullivan, L H, *The autobiography of an idea*, New York 1956, 324-5.

157 Anthony Caro, quoted in Compton, S, editor, *British art in the 20th century: the modern movement*, (exhibition, London, Royal Academy), London and Munich 1986, 43, and note 48. See also 'Anthony Caro talks about Henry Moore', *Modern Painters* 1.3, 1988, 7-13.

158 Rosenblum, R, in Compton 1986, 89: in his essay (89-98), Rosenblum perceives a strong Romantic and 19th-century vein in British 20th-century art.

159 Sylvester, D, *Henry Moore* (exhibition, Tate Gallery), London 1968, 35.

160 Sylvester, *op cit*, 6; from an article in *The Listener* XIII, 334, 5 June 1935, 944.

161 Holt, E, *A documentary history of art*, III, New York 1966, 523-4.

162 Reff, T, 'Cézanne and Poussin', *JWCI* XXIII.1-2, 1960, 150-74.

163 Hamilton, G H, *Painting and sculpture in Europe, 1880-1940*, Harmondsworth 1967, 305, 304.

164 Jencks 1987, 127, 151.

165 Survey in Sloane, J C, *French painting between the past and the present: artists, critics and traditions from 1848 to 1870*, Princeton NJ 1951.

166 Elsen, A E, *Rodin and Balzac* (exhibition, Stanford Univ), Beverly Hills, 1973.

167 Pommer, R, 'Modernism, revisionism, pluralism and post-modernism', *Art Journal* 40.1/2, 1980, 353-61: see 360.

168 C Jameson, in a review of Bruno Zevi's *The modern language of architecture* in *Jnl Society of Architectural Historians* XL:1, March 1981, 80. See generally Curtis, W J R, *Modern architecture since 1900*, Oxford 1982; and Gale, A, 'Mies van der Rohe: an appreciation' in *Mies van der Rohe: European Works*, Architectural Monographs 11, London 1986, 95-9, with good bibliography.

169  For the broader picture, see Banham, R, *Theory and design of the first machine age*, London 1960, eg 44-67.

170  Le Corbusier, *Towards a new architecture*, Eng trans, London 1946, 266.

171  Stern, R A M, *Modern classicism*, London 1988; Smith, T G, *Classical architecture: rule and invention*, Layton, Utah 1988.

172  Wigley, M, in the exhibition catalogue *Deconstructivist architecture*, MoMA, New York 1988, 16.

173  For this building in its context, see Brawne, M, *The new museum: architecture and display*, New York 1965, 119-20: see 136f for Mies' Museum of Fine Arts in Houston, of 1958; and 138-41 for Johnson's Miesian Museum of Art at Utica, of 1960.

174  details in Brawne 1965, 146-8.

175  Scully, V, *American architecture and urbanism*, London 1969, 184.

176  Filler, M, 'Building and nothingness', review of recent publications on Mies (and a good *tour d'horizon*) in *The New York Review of Books*, XXXIII.10, 1986, 26-33: see 26.

177  Rowe, C, 'Neo-"classicism" and modern architecture', reprinted in *The mathematics of the ideal villa*, Cambridge MA & London 1976, 120-38 & 140-58.

178  Van Leeuwen, T A P, *The skyward trend of thought: the metaphysics of the American skyscraper*, Cambridge MA 1988.

179  Dorrdan, D P, 'The political content in Italian architecture during the Fascist era', *Art Journal* 43.2, 1983, 121-31; Kopp, A, *Town and revolution: Soviet architecture and city planning, 1917-1935*, New York 1970; Nilsson, N A, editor, *Art, society, revolution: Russia, 1917-1921*, Stockholm 1979 (Stockholm Studies in Russian Literature, 11).

180  Lancaster, O, *Pillar to post. The pocket lamp of architecture*, London 1938, 78.

181  Warnke, M, editor, *Politische Architektur in Europe von Mittelalter bis heute: Repraesentation und Gemeinschaft*, Cologne 1984; Taylor, R R, *The word in stone. The role of architecture in the National Socialist ideology*, Berkeley & London 1974; Duffler J, *et al. Hitlers Staedte. Baupolitik im Dritten Reich. Eine Dokumentation*, Cologne & Vienna 1978.

182  Wulf, J, *Die bildende Kuenste in Dritten Reich*, Goetesloh 1963, pl 30.

183  Herf, J, *Reactionary modernism: technology, culture, and politics in Weimar and the Third Reich*, Cambridge & New York 1984; Warner, B, 'Berlin – the Nordic homeland and the corruption of urban spectacle', in Clelland, D, ed, *Berlin: an architectural history (AD Profile)*, London 1983, 73-88.

184  Fried, R C, *Planning the Eternal City. Roman politics and planning since World War II*, New Haven & London 1973: quotation from 33; Cederna, A, *Mussolini urbanista: Lo sventramento di Roma negli anni di consenso*, Bari 1980. Vol 43.2 for 1983 of *The Art Journal* is devoted to the theme of *revising modernist history: the architecture of the 1920s and 1930s:* see eg Doordan, D P, 'The political content in Italian architecture during the Fascist era', 121-31.

185  Speer, A, *Inside the Third Reich*. Eng trans New York 1970; review by B Miller Lane in JSAH XXXII.4, 1973, 3416.

186  Krier, L, 'An architecture of desire', *Architectural Design* 56, 4, 1986, 31-7: see 31; also Krier, L, editor *Albert Speer: Architecture 1932-42* (Archives d'Architécture Moderne), Brussels 1985.

187  Jencks, *The Language of Post-Modern Architecture*, New York 1984, 20.

188  Fokkema, D W, *Literary history, modernism, and postmodernism*, Amsterdam 1984 (Utrecht publications in general and comparative literature, 19); Fokkema D W, and Bertens, H, editors, *Workshop on Postmodernism: approaching postmodernism* (Conference, University of Utrecht, 1984), Amsterdam 1986 (Utrecht Publications in General and Comparative Literature, 21).

189  Benhabib, S, 'Epistemologies of Postmodernism: a rejoinder to Jean-François Lyotard', *New German Critique* 33 1984, 103-26; Fuller, P, *Aesthetics after modernism*, London 1983.

190  Jencks, C, 'Late modernism vs post-modernism: the two-party system', *Journal of Architectural Theory and Criticism* 1.1, 1988, 27-39: see 278; and 39 for a chart detailing his view of the ideological, stylistic and design characteristics of modern, late-modern and postmodern architecture. The bibliography on post-modernism is large, and growing: see also Jencks' *What is post-modernism?*, 2nd rev. and enl. ed., London 1987, and also his *Post-modernism: the new classicism in art and architecture*, London 1987. The *Art Journal* 40.1-2, 1980, is dedicated to *Modernism, revisionism, pluralism and post-modernism; Les Cahiers du Musée National d'Art Moderne* 22, 1987, is devoted to the subject of *Aprés le modernisme:* see Torres, F, 'Métamoderne: remarques à propos d'une nouvelle querelle des Anciens et des Modernes', 19-31. Other useful works include: Stern 1988; Trachtenberg, S, *The Postmodern moment: a handbook of contemporary innovation in the arts*, Westport, Conn. 1985.

191  Frampton, K, 'Place-form and cultural identity', in Thackara, J, ed, *Design after modernity*, London 1988, 51-66. See 62ff, he suggests markers for distinguishing between anti-modernists (as he labels the historicists) and post-modernists.

192  McLeod, M, 'Architecture', in Trachtenberg 1985, 19-52, with excellent bibliography: see 19 for quote. This is echoed by C Dinot in his review 'What is the Post-Modern?', *Art History* 9.2, 1986, 245-63: see 250. See also: Gablik, S, *Has modernism failed?*, New York, 1984; *The new modernism: deconstructionist tendancies in art*, London 1988 (*Art and Design* Profiles, 8) Wallis, B, editor, *Art after modernism: rethinking representation*, New York etc. 1984 (Documentary Sources in Contemporary Art, 1); Fekete, J, editor, *Life after postmodernism: essays on value and culture*, New York 1987.

193  Jencks 1984.

194  Hall, P, *Cities of tomorrow. An intellectual history of urban planning and design in the 20th century*, Oxford 1988, 5.

195  Jencks 1984, 21ff.

196  Russell, C, *Poets, prophets and revolutionaries: the literary avant-garde from Rimbaud through Postmodernism*, New York 1985.

197  Benton, T & C, *Form and function: a source book for the history of architecture and design 1890-1939*, London 1975; Hersey, G, *The lost meaning of classical architecture. Speculations on ornament from Vitruvius to Venturi*, Cambridge, Mass., 1988.

198  Jensen, R, and Conway, P, *Ornamentalism*, New York 1982, 1.

199  Fuller, 'The search for a postmodern aesthetic', Thackara 1988, 117-34: see 117.

200  P Goldberger in the foreword to Jensen & Conway 1982, xiii.

201  B Zevi in a discussion entitled 'Is Post-Modern architecture serious?', *Architectural Design* 52, 1/2, 1982, 20.

202  In a review of Aslet, *Quinlan Terry: the revival of architecture*, and other books, in *The New York Review of Books*, XXXV.14, September 1988, 27-33: see 28.

203  Blundell Jones, P, 'Richmond Riverside: sugaring the pill', *Architectural Review* CLXXXIV, November 1988, 87-90: see 90.

204  Bruno Zevi in *Architectural Design* 52 1/2 1982, 21.

205  Moore, C, 'You've got to pay for the public life', *Perspecta* 9/10, 1964, 57-106; cf the comments in Pommer 1980, 354f.

206  Klotz 1985, 35.

207  Porphyrios 1984, 30.

208  The best case for the prosecution is presented in a thoughtful piece by Demetri Porphyrios, 'Building and architecture', *AD* 54, 5/6, 1984, 7-9, 30-1.

209  Middleton, R, 'Disintegration', *Architectural design* XXXVII.7, 1967, 204; cited by D Porphyrios, *Architectural Design* 52, 1/2, 1982, 3.

210  cf Huyssen 1986, especially 178-221, *Mapping the Post-Modern:* he writes (184) of the 'gesture of random historical citation which prevails on so many postmodern façades'.

211  Bragdon, C, 'The language of form', in Mumford *op cit*, 358-68: see 364.

212  Cass, C, *Grand illusions: contemporary interior murals*, Oxford 1988; Milman, M, *Trompe l'oeil painted architecture*, New York 1986; ibid., *Trompe l'oeil painting: the illusions of reality*, Geneva & London 1983.

213  Nairne 1987, 30.

214  Gregory, A, *Modern Painters* 1.1, 1988, 96-7.

215  Quoted in McHale, B, *Postmodernist fiction*, New York & London 1987, 3.

216  Trachtenberg, M, Some observations on recent architectural history', *Art Bulletin* LXX.2, 1988, 208-41: see 225.

217 Hall 1988, 204-40. See 204: 'The evil that le Corbusier did lives after him . . . Ideas, forged in the Parisian intelligentsia of the 1920s, came to be applied to the planning of working-class housing . . . the results were at best questionable, at worst catastrophic.'

218 Venturi, R, *Complexity and contradiction in architecture*, rev ed, New York 1977, 18-19.

219 Eisenman, P, editor, *Philip Johnson: writings*, New York 1979, 268, 165, 271.

220 Venturi, 1977, 50.

221 Fuller, P, in Thackara 1988, 128.

222 Johnson, P, Introduction to the exhibition on *Deconstructivist architecture*, MoMA, New York 1988, 8.

223 *Architectural Design* 52 1/2 1982 (edited by C Jencks), in a discussion of the Venice *Biennale*, 8-9.

224 Venturi, 1977, 14.

225 Dunster, ed, *Michael Graves*, Architectural Monographs 5, London 1979, 26f.

226 In his *The language of post-modern architecture*, rev ed, London 1978, 64. See also Klotz, H, *The history of postmodern architecture*, Eng trans London 1988, 324ff; for plentiful examples of twenties influence, see Jencks, C, 'Twenties revivalism' in his *Architecture today*, rev ed, London 1988 74-89.

227 Bruno Zevi in *Architectural Design* 52 1/2 1982, 7, 20-1. As an example, see Porphyrios' 1987 house in Kensington (*Architectural Design* 58, 1/2, 1988, 70-7) which is traditional neo-Greek of the Schliemann variety, crossed with a standard Georgian terrace.

228 Ryckwert, J, 'The Ecole des Beaux Arts and the classical tradition', in Middleton, R, ed, *The Beaux Arts and 19th-century French architecture*, London 1982, 8-17; see 17: EBA 'is an all-too-solid monument to the classical tradition'.

229 Twombly, R, editor, *Louis Sullivan, the public papers*, Chicago & London 1988, 123-5; see 124.

230 Twombly, op.cit., 140 & 178-9, in papers given in 1900 and 1906.

231 Zevi, B, *The modern language of architecture*, Canberra 1978, 116-16.

232 North, A T ed, *Ralph Adams Cram*, NY & London 1931, quotes from pp 3, 8.

233 In Stern, RAM, *New directions in American architecture*, New York 1969, 51.

234 Colquhoun, A, in Dunster 1979, 8-17, for comments on Graves & Ledoux.

235 'The National Gallery', *AD* 56, 1/2, 1986, provides an interim report.

236 Klotz, H, ed, 'Revision of the Modern' in *Architectural Design* 55, 3/4, 1985, 62.

237 See also Venturi, Rauch & Scott Brown's house in New Castle County, Delaware, of 1982, which uses a similar motif.

238 Scully 1969 for model and plan.

239 Frampton, K, 'Place-form and cultural identity', in Thackara 1988: see 54.

240 Greehalgh, M, *Bernini and the City of Rome*, Sydney 1988, 7-11, 18-25.

241 Editorial comment in the *Architectural Review*, CLXXXII, Nov 1987, 74-7.

242 Altieri, C. 'John Ashbery and the challenge of Postmodernism in the visual arts,' *Critical Inquiry* 14.4, 1988, 805-30. See 805: 'By banishing writers like Ashbery to literary tradition, we leave the domain of the postmodern to two dominant discourses. One is driven by post-structural theory's idealisation of the nomadic, the undecidable, and the profusion of simulacra. The other champions Marxist values which cast as the most significant contemporary art the rather slight oppositional devices of artists like Sherrie Levine, Hans Haacke, and Barbara Kruger . . . does the age demand the emergence of a new sensibility, strands of which are being woven in post-structuralist mills?'

243 In an interview in *Architectural Design* 52, 1/2, 1982, 17.

244 cf Harries, K, 'Modernity's bad conscience in *AA Files* (Annals of the Architectural Association School of Architecture) 10, 1985, 53-60. See 54 on postmodernism as the new Humanism: 'does such rhetoric not misrepresent postmodernism by taking it more seriously than it deserves . . . by tranforming itself into post-modern neoclassicism, post-modernism has degenerated into a new

orthodoxy . . . it has become boring.'

245 eg Collins, M, *Towards post-modernism: design since 1851*, London 1987; Trachtenberg, M, & Hyman, I, *Architecture: from prehistory to post-modernism: the Western tradition*, London 1986.

246 Papadakis, A, 'Post-Modern Classicism', *Architectural Design* 5/6, 1980, 68.

247 cf comments in Nairne, S, *State of the art: ideas and images in the 1980s*, London 1987, 19ff.

248 'Post-Modern Classicism', *AD* 5/6, 1980, 5, his *Introduction* to the volume.

249 *ibid*, 16.

250 Porphyrios, D, 'Classicism is not a style', *Architectural Design* 52, 5/6, 1982, 51-7: see 52 & 53. This is almost a definition of airport art.

251 Certainly not literature: cf. Huyssen, A, *After the great divide: modernism, mass culture, postmodernism*, Bloomington IN 1986.

252 Tafuri, M, *The sphere and the labyrinth. Avant-gardes and architecture from Piranesi to the 1970s*, Eng trans Cambridge, Mass and London 1987; eg 296: 'rarified and precious compositions . . . a group of incurable snobs, bent on catering to the most elite tendencies of the affluent society'.

253 Jameson, F, 'The politics of theory: ideological positions in the Postmodernism debate', *New German Critique* 33 1984, 53-65: see 63-4.

254 Hersey 1988, 155-6.

255 Goldberger, P, 'In perpetuum', *Architectural Record* 174, April 1986, 172ff.

256 Brendel, O J, *The visible idea. Interpretations of classical art*, Washington DC, 1980; Oates, W J, *From Sophocles to Picasso: the present-day vitality of the classical tradition*, Bloomington, Ind, 1964.

257 Scruton, R, *The aesthetics of architecture*, London 1979, 226: *Style is not the accumulation of detail, but its fitting deployment.*

258 Cf *Roma antiqua. Forum, Colisée, Palatin. Envois des architectes français (1788-1924)* (exhibition, Rome & Paris), Rome 1985; see also Hellmann M C, & Fraisse, P, 'Architecture grècque et envois de Rome: historique et tendance', in *Paris-Rome-Athènes: Le voyage en Grèce des architectes français aux XIXe et XXe siècles*, (Exhibition, Paris, Athens, Houston, New York), 2nd ed., Paris 1983, 25-38: *L'architecture antique est en train de redevenir ce qu'elle a ete pendant des siècles, un des ferments de la création architecturale, apres deux ou trois décennies d'amnésie ou les architectes avaient crus pouvoir s'en passer. Dans le grand débat de l'architecture contemporaine, les Envois de Rome consacrés à l'antiquité grècque ont bel et bien leur role à jouer – although the authors do not say how.

259 D'Amato, C, 'Villa Adriana: la costruzione dell'architettura e la memoria', in Paris, T, editor, *L'antico come luogo della memoria*, Rome 1984, 48-67: comparanda are the Salk Institute at La Jolla for Kahn; Frank Lloyd Wright's Southern College project of the late 1930s; and the tower over the SW chapel at Ronchamp, for which d'Amico adduces Le Corbusier's drawing of the apse of the Canopus.

260 *RIBA Jnl*, September 1977, 366-7).

261 Quoted in Jencks, C, 'Philip Johnson, the candid King Midas of New York camp', in *Late modern architecture*, New York 1980, 146-59: see 154.

262 Taylor, B B, 'Rethinking colonial architecture', *Mimar: Architecture in Development* 13, 1984, 16-25: see 16.

263 This is the theme of *Mimar* 19, 1986.

264 Taylor 1984, 22.

265 Curtis, W J R, 'Modernism and the search for Indian identity', *Architectural review* CLXXXII, August 1987, 32-8: see 37.

266 Taylor, B B, 'Perspectives and limits on regionalism and architectural identity' in *Mimar* 19, 1986, 19-21: see 20.

267 Ravindran, K T, *Architectural Review* CLXXXII, August 1987, 63.

268 Jencks 1988, 312.

269 Radin, *loc cit*, 67.

———— * ————